So You've Been Baptized, What's Next: The Road to Discipleship

Minister Jeremy B. Sims

Published by Jeremy Sims, 2023.

While every precaution has been taken in the preparation of this book, the publisher assumes no responsibility for errors or omissions, or for damages resulting from the use of the information contained herein.

SO YOU'VE BEEN BAPTIZED, WHAT'S NEXT: THE ROAD TO DISCIPLESHIP

First edition. September 14, 2023.

ISBN: 979-8223968931

Written by Minister Jeremy B. Sims.

Also by Minister Jeremy B. Sims

Stop Blaming the Adversary: It's You!
From Milk to Meat: The Journey of Spiritual Maturity
So You've Been Baptized, What's Next: The Road to Discipleship
Why Worrying is A Waste: The Biblical Perspective

Introduction

CONGRATULATIONS ON taking the important step of baptism! Baptism is a beautiful and meaningful expression of your faith in Jesus Christ, symbolizing your identification with His death, burial, and resurrection. It marks the beginning of your journey as a disciple of Jesus. But what's next? How do you continue to grow in your faith and deepen your relationship with God? This book, "So You've Been Baptized, What's Next: The Road to Discipleship," is here to guide you on your path.

Chapter 1: The Significance of Baptism

BAPTISM IS NOT JUST a ritual; it's a profound and meaningful expression of your faith in Jesus Christ. In this chapter, we will delve into the deep significance of baptism and why it holds a special place in the life of a Christian.

The Symbolism of Baptism

At its core, baptism is a symbol. It represents a powerful message that is central to the Christian faith. When you are baptized, you are symbolically participating in three significant events:

Death and Burial: Baptism symbolizes your identification with the death and burial of Jesus Christ. Just as Jesus died on the cross for the forgiveness of sins and was buried, your immersion in the water signifies a burial of your old self, with its sins and brokenness. Romans 6:4 explains, "We were buried therefore with him by baptism into death, in order that, just as Christ was raised from the dead by the glory of the Father, we too might walk in newness of life."

Resurrection: Baptism also symbolizes your identification with the resurrection of Jesus. As you rise out of the water, it represents your new life in Christ. You are no longer bound by the power of sin but have been raised to walk in the newness of life. Colossians 2:12 reinforces this concept: "having been buried with him in baptism, in which you were also raised with him through faith in the powerful working of God, who raised him from the dead."

CLEANSING AND FORGIVENESS: Baptism serves as a symbol of cleansing and forgiveness. It represents the washing away of your sins and impurities, as you surrender your life to Christ. Acts 22:16 highlights this symbolism: "And now why do you wait? Rise and be baptized and wash away your sins, calling on his name."

Through these symbolic acts of baptism, you publicly declare your faith in Jesus Christ and your commitment to follow Him. It's a powerful initiation into the family of believers and a reminder of the transformative power of Christ's death and resurrection in your life.

Baptism as an Act of Obedience

Baptism is not an optional extra for Christians; it is a commandment given by Jesus Himself. In Matthew 28:19-20, known as the Great Commission, Jesus instructs His disciples to baptize new believers in the name of the Father, Son, and Holy Spirit. By obeying this command, you are demonstrating your submission to Christ's lordship and your willingness to follow His teachings.

The Great Commission: The Great Commission is a foundational directive for all believers. Jesus' words in Matthew 28:19-20 are clear: "Go therefore and make disciples of all nations, baptizing them in the name of the Father and of the Son and of the Holy Spirit, teaching them to observe all that I have commanded you."

An Act of Submission: Baptism is an act of obedience that signifies your submission to Christ's lordship. It's a tangible way to demonstrate that you are placing your life under His authority and acknowledging Him as your Savior and Lord.

Identifying with Christ: When you obey the command to be baptized, you are identifying with the life, death, and resurrection of Jesus Christ. Just as He was obedient to the Father's will, you are obedient to His command to be baptized.

An Essential Step: Baptism is a crucial step in the journey of faith. It is the initial public declaration of your faith in Christ and your commitment to follow Him. It marks the beginning of your discipleship journey.

A Symbol of Regeneration: Baptism symbolizes the regeneration and transformation that occurs when you surrender your life to Christ. It signifies the washing away of sin and the emergence of a new creation in Christ.

By obeying Christ's command to be baptized, you not only align yourself with His teachings but also become a participant in the unfolding narrative of God's redemptive plan. Baptism is an act of faith, obedience, and proclamation—an outward expression of your inward commitment to follow Jesus and be part of His kingdom.

An Outward Expression of an Inner Faith

Your baptism is a public declaration of your faith in Jesus Christ. It is a way of proclaiming to the world that you have chosen to follow Him and be His disciple. It's a visible testimony of your inner transformation and your decision to live a life that reflects His teachings.

A Public Proclamation: Baptism is not a private affair but a public proclamation of your faith. By undergoing this act, you openly declare your commitment to Jesus as your Lord and Savior.

Identifying with Christ: Through baptism, you identify with the life, death, and resurrection of Jesus. Just as He willingly laid down His life for you, you willingly surrender your life to Him.

A Witness to Others: Your baptism serves as a witness to others. It communicates to those around you that you are a follower of Jesus and that your life is now defined by His teachings.

A Visual Representation: Baptism visually represents the transformation that has occurred within you. You go into the water symbolizing your old life, and you emerge from it as a new creation in Christ (2 Corinthians 5:17).

A Step of Faith: Baptism is a step of faith that marks the beginning of your discipleship journey. It's a concrete way to express your trust in God's promises and your desire to walk in obedience to Him.

Reflecting His Teachings: As you are baptized and continue your discipleship journey, you commit to living a life that reflects the teachings of Jesus. You become a living example of His love, grace, and truth.

Your baptism is a profound moment in your faith journey—a moment of commitment, transformation, and public witness. It reminds you that faith is not merely a private matter but a dynamic relationship with Jesus that is meant to be shared with the world. Through baptism, you declare to all that you are His disciple, seeking to live in His ways and bring glory to His name.

A STEP TOWARD DISCIPLESHIP

Baptism is not the end of your journey; it's the beginning. It's the first step on the road to discipleship. It signifies your commitment to walk in the footsteps of Jesus, learn from His teachings, and grow in your relationship with Him.

In this chapter, we have explored the rich symbolism of baptism and its significance in the life of a Christian. It is more than just a ritual; it is a profound expression of faith, obedience to Christ's command, and a declaration of your commitment to the path of discipleship. As we continue on this journey, remember that baptism is a starting point—an exciting step towards a life dedicated to following Jesus and becoming His disciple.

Chapter 2: The Foundation of Discipleship

IN THIS CHAPTER, WE will explore the critical elements that form the foundation of your journey as a disciple of Jesus. Just as a strong foundation is essential for a sturdy building, these foundational aspects of discipleship are crucial for your spiritual growth and endurance.

The Role of Prayer

Prayer is your direct line of communication with God. It is the cornerstone of your relationship with Him. Through prayer, you can:

Seek Guidance: Regular prayer allows you to seek God's guidance in your daily decisions and challenges. You can bring your concerns, hopes, and dreams before Him, knowing that He hears and cares for you.

Express Gratitude: Gratitude is a powerful aspect of prayer. Taking time to thank God for His blessings fosters a spirit of contentment and humility.

Expressing Thankfulness:

Count Your Blessings: Begin your prayers by counting your blessings. Reflect on the many ways God has provided for you, protected you, and shown His love in your life.

Specific Thanks: Be specific in your expressions of gratitude. Instead of generic thanksgiving, offer thanks for moments, people, or circumstances that have touched your life.

Humble Acknowledgment: Expressing gratitude is a humble acknowledgment that you are reliant on God's goodness and grace. It reminds you that all you have comes from His hand.

Contentment: Gratitude fosters contentment. By focusing on what you have rather than what you lack, you can experience a deeper sense of peace and satisfaction.

A Grateful Heart: Cultivate a grateful heart in your prayers. Recognize that every day is filled with opportunities to be thankful and express your gratitude in both the big and small moments of life.

Thanksgiving in All Circumstances: Even in difficult times or moments of suffering, find reasons to be thankful. This doesn't mean you have to be thankful for the pain but for God's presence and His ability to work through challenging situations.

The Power of Gratitude in Prayer:

Deepens Your Relationship: Gratitude in prayer deepens your relationship with God. It allows you to approach Him not only with requests but also with a heart full of appreciation.

Fosters Joy: Gratitude is often linked to joy. When you acknowledge and thank God for His blessings, you experience a sense of joy and contentment that transcends your circumstances.

Shifts Perspective: Gratitude shifts your perspective. It helps you focus on the positive aspects of life and reminds you of God's faithfulness, even during challenges.

Strengthens Faith: A grateful heart strengthens your faith. It reminds you of God's past provision and assures you that He will continue to care for you in the future.

Inspires Generosity: Gratitude often inspires generosity. As you recognize God's blessings, you may be more inclined to share your blessings with others.

Incorporating gratitude into your prayers is a beautiful way to draw closer to God and cultivate a spirit of contentment and joy in your life. It's a practice that aligns your heart with His and helps you recognize the abundance of His blessings, both seen and unseen.

Confession and Repentance: Through prayer, you can honestly acknowledge your sins and seek forgiveness. It is a vital part of staying spiritually clean and growing in your relationship with God.

Confession:

Honest Self-Examination: Begin by honestly examining your heart and actions. Confession involves acknowledging your sins and shortcomings before God.

Specific Confession: Be specific in your confession. Name the sins and areas where you have fallen short. This specificity allows you to address your shortcomings directly.

Sincere Regret: Approach confession with sincere regret for your sins. Recognize the impact of your actions on your relationship with God and others.

Request Forgiveness: Confession includes asking God for forgiveness. Remember that God is merciful and willing to forgive when you come to Him with a repentant heart.

Forgiving Others: As you confess your sins, consider any grievances you hold against others and forgive them. Jesus emphasized the importance of forgiveness in the Lord's Prayer (Matthew 6:12).

Repentance:

Turning Away from Sin: Repentance involves a deliberate turning away from sin and a commitment to live according to God's principles. It's not merely feeling sorry for your sins but taking action to change.

Seek God's Help: Acknowledge your need for God's help in overcoming sin. Repentance is not a solo effort but a partnership with God's transforming grace.

Developing a Plan: If you struggle with specific sins or patterns of behavior, develop a plan to avoid temptation and seek accountability from a trusted friend or mentor.

Cultivating Virtue: Repentance is not just about avoiding sin but also about cultivating virtues and Christ-like character. Strive to replace sinful habits with godly ones.

THE POWER OF CONFESSION and Repentance in Prayer:

Restored Relationship: Confession and repentance mend your relationship with God. They open the way for restoration and renewal of your spiritual intimacy with Him.

Spiritual Cleansing: Confession and repentance spiritually cleanse you, removing the barriers that hinder your fellowship with God.

Growth in Holiness: Engaging in these practices leads to growth in holiness. As you continually confess and repent, you become more like Christ.

Freedom from Guilt: Confession and repentance free you from the burden of guilt and shame. They allow you to experience the fullness of God's forgiveness and grace.

Ongoing Transformation: Regular confession and repentance are vital for ongoing spiritual transformation. They help you identify areas in need of growth and invite God to work in your life.

Remember that confession and repentance are not a one-time event but a lifelong practice for every believer. They enable you to maintain a humble and contrite heart, continuously drawing closer to God and growing in His grace and holiness.

Intercession:

Praying for others is an essential part of discipleship. It allows you to show love and compassion for those around you, just as Jesus did.

INTERCESSORY PRAYER:

Identifying Needs: Begin by identifying the needs of others. Pay attention to the challenges, struggles, and concerns that your friends, family, community, and even strangers may be facing.

Specific Intercession: Be specific in your intercessory prayers. Name individuals or situations that require God's intervention and offer heartfelt petitions on their behalf.

Empathy and Compassion: Approach intercessory prayer with empathy and compassion. Try to understand the emotions and experiences of those you are praying for.

Praying for Enemies: Jesus encouraged His followers to pray for their enemies (Matthew 5:44). Include those who have wronged you or whom you find difficult to love in your intercessory prayers.

Faith and Expectation: Pray with faith and expectation, trusting that God hears and responds to your intercessions. James 5:16 reminds you, "The prayer of a righteous person has great power."

The Power of Intercession in Discipleship:

Demonstrates Love: Intercessory prayer is a tangible expression of love for others. It shows that you care deeply about their well-being and spiritual growth.

Strengthens Relationships: Praying for others strengthens your relationships with them. It fosters a sense of unity and support within your faith community and among your loved ones.

Brings Comfort: Your intercessory prayers can bring comfort and peace to those you pray for. It reminds them that they are not alone in their struggles.

Invites God's Intervention: Intercession invites God's intervention and guidance into the lives of those you pray for. It acknowledges that you trust in His sovereign power.

Reflects Christ's Heart: Intercession reflects the heart of Jesus, who interceded for His disciples and all believers (John 17:20-26). It aligns your heart with His mission of love and redemption.

Develops Empathy: Regular intercessory prayer deepens your empathy for others. It helps you see the world from different perspectives and prompts you to act with compassion.

Intercession is a powerful and transformative practice that not only benefits those you pray for but also enriches your own discipleship journey. It encourages you to extend love, grace, and care to a hurting world, demonstrating the love of Christ in tangible ways.

The Role of Scripture

The Bible is your guidebook for discipleship. It is God's Word, filled with wisdom, guidance, and revelation. In your journey as a disciple, you can rely on the Bible to:

Know God: The Bible reveals God's character, His promises, and His will for your life. Through it, you can deepen your understanding of who God is.

KNOWING GOD THROUGH Scripture:

1. **Exploring His Character:** The Bible provides a comprehensive portrait of God's character. You can learn about His attributes such as love, mercy, justice, and faithfulness through the stories, teachings, and descriptions found in Scripture.

Discovering His Promises: God's promises are scattered throughout the Bible. As you read and study, you'll come across promises that offer hope, guidance, and assurance in various situations.

Understanding His Will: Scripture reveals God's will for your life. It contains principles and guidance that can help you make decisions aligned with His purposes.

Seeing His Actions: The stories in the Bible illustrate God's actions in the lives of individuals, nations, and the world. These narratives provide insight into how God interacts with humanity.

Learning from His Wisdom: The Bible is filled with wisdom for daily living. It offers guidance on topics like relationships, morality, finances, and purpose.

Deepening Your Understanding:

Regular Reading: Make reading the Bible a regular habit. Set aside time each day to engage with God's Word, allowing it to speak to your heart and mind.

Study and Meditation: Go beyond reading by studying Scripture in-depth. Use study Bibles, commentaries, and study guides to help you delve into the meaning and context of passages. Meditation on Scripture allows you to internalize its teachings and apply them to your life.

Prayerful Reflection: Pray as you read and study the Bible. Ask God to reveal Himself to you and to help you understand His Word.

Seeking Guidance: If you encounter passages that are difficult to understand, seek guidance from trusted mentors, pastors, or scholars. Don't be afraid to ask questions and engage in discussions.

Application: Apply what you learn from Scripture to your life. Seek to live out the principles and teachings you discover.

The Power of Knowing God:

Deepens Your Relationship: Knowing God through His Word deepens your relationship with Him. It's a way of drawing closer to the One who created and loves you.

Strengthens Your Faith: Understanding who God is and His faithfulness throughout history strengthens your faith. It provides a foundation for trust and confidence in Him.

Guides Your Decisions: Scripture offers guidance for making decisions in line with God's will. It can help you navigate life's challenges and choices.

Transforms Your Character: The more you know God, the more you become like Him. His character begins to shape your own, producing the fruits of the Spirit in your life.

Provides Comfort and Encouragement: In times of difficulty, the truths you've learned from Scripture can bring comfort and encouragement. They remind you of God's presence and His promises.

Getting to know God through the Bible is an ongoing, lifelong journey. As you deepen your understanding of who He is, you'll find that your faith grows stronger, your relationship with Him becomes richer, and your life is transformed in profound ways.

Understand Truth:

It provides a solid foundation of truth that helps you discern right from wrong and make wise decisions.

The Role of Truth in Scripture:

Moral and Ethical Guidance: The Bible contains clear moral and ethical principles that serve as a guide for your conduct and decision-making. It defines what is right and wrong in the sight of God.

Spiritual Wisdom: Scripture imparts spiritual wisdom and discernment, enabling you to navigate complex moral and ethical dilemmas in a way that aligns with God's values.

Truth About God: The Bible reveals the truth about God's character, His love, and His redemptive plan. This knowledge helps you make decisions that reflect His will.

Truth About Humanity: Scripture provides insights into the human condition, helping you understand your own nature, struggles, and potential for growth.

Discerning Right from Wrong:

Study and Reflection: Regularly studying and reflecting on Scripture equips you with the knowledge of God's truth. When faced with decisions, you can turn to these principles for guidance.

Prayerful Consideration: Seek God's guidance in prayer when you encounter challenging choices. Ask Him to illuminate His truth and will as you make decisions.

Seeking Counsel: Seek counsel from wise and spiritually mature individuals within your faith community. They can help you apply biblical principles to specific situations.

Testing Against Scripture: When making decisions, test them against the truths found in the Bible. Ask whether your choices align with God's revealed will and moral standards.

The Power of Understanding Truth:

Moral Clarity: Understanding truth from Scripture provides moral clarity in a world where values and ethics can be subjective and shifting.

Consistency in Decision-Making: A foundation of truth ensures consistency in your decision-making, helping you avoid making choices based solely on emotions or cultural trends.

Strengthens Character: Embracing biblical truth shapes your character and fosters a commitment to living a life of integrity and righteousness.

Aids in Resisting Temptation: Knowing the truth helps you resist temptation and make choices that honor God, even when faced with pressure to compromise.

Peace and Confidence: Understanding truth brings a sense of peace and confidence in your decisions, knowing you are following the path that aligns with God's will.

Wise Choices: A foundation of truth equips you to make wise choices that lead to blessings and spiritual growth.

Incorporating biblical truth into your decision-making process is essential for living a life that honors God and aligns with His values. It provides a solid moral compass and empowers you to navigate life's complexities with wisdom and discernment.

Grow Spiritually:

Regularly reading and studying the Bible nourishes your spirit, strengthens your faith, and equips you for the challenges you may face.

Spiritual Growth Through Scripture:

Nourishing Your Spirit: Just as your physical body needs regular nourishment, your spirit requires spiritual nourishment. The Bible provides the sustenance your soul needs to thrive.

Deepening Your Faith: Regular engagement with Scripture deepens your faith. It reinforces the foundational truths of your belief and strengthens your trust in God.

Spiritual Transformation: As you immerse yourself in God's Word, it has the power to transform your heart and mind. Romans 12:2 encourages you to be "transformed by the renewal of your mind."

Equipping for Challenges: Scripture equips you for the challenges of life. It provides wisdom, guidance, and encouragement when facing trials and uncertainties.

Cultivating Spiritual Growth:

Consistent Reading: Make reading the Bible a consistent part of your daily routine. Whether it's a few verses or entire chapters, the regularity of reading matters.

Study and Reflection: Delve deeper into Scripture through study and reflection. Use study Bibles, commentaries, and devotionals to gain insights into the text.

Meditation: Meditation on Scripture involves pondering its meaning and relevance in your life. Take time to let the words of the Bible sink into your heart and soul.

Application: Apply the teachings of the Bible to your life. Seek to live out its principles, values, and commands in your daily actions and decisions.

Group Study: Participate in group Bible studies or discussions within your faith community. Engaging with others can provide different perspectives and deepen your understanding.

The Power of Spiritual Growth Through Scripture:

Increased Knowledge of God: Regular engagement with the Bible leads to a deeper knowledge of God, His character, and His ways.

Strengthened Faith: As you grow spiritually, your faith is strengthened, making you more resilient in the face of challenges and doubts.

Character Transformation: The Bible has the power to transform your character, producing the fruits of the Spirit, such as love, joy, peace, patience, and self-control (Galatians 5:22-23).

Guidance and Wisdom: Scripture provides guidance and wisdom for navigating life's complexities and making decisions that honor God.

Empowerment: As you grow spiritually, you are empowered to live out your faith more boldly and authentically, becoming a living testimony of God's grace.

Spiritual Resilience: Spiritual growth through Scripture equips you to withstand trials and temptations, drawing strength from your deepening relationship with God.

Regularly engaging with the Bible is a cornerstone of spiritual growth and discipleship. It nourishes your spirit, deepens your faith, and empowers you to live a life that reflects the teachings of Jesus Christ.

The Role of Community

Discipleship is not a solo journey. It's essential to connect with a faith community, such as a church or small group. Here's how a faith community can contribute to your foundation:

Support and Accountability: Fellow believers can provide support, encouragement, and accountability as you walk the path of discipleship. They can help you stay on course and lift you up in times of struggle.

The Importance of Support and Accountability:

Spiritual Encouragement: Fellow believers can encourage and uplift you in your faith journey. They can share their own experiences, offer prayers, and provide emotional support during challenging times.

Shared Experiences: Discipleship is often easier when it's shared. Fellow disciples can relate to your struggles and victories, creating a sense of camaraderie and understanding.

Accountability: Having people who hold you accountable in your walk with God can help you stay committed to your spiritual disciplines and values.

Guidance and Mentorship: More experienced disciples can offer guidance and mentorship, helping you navigate unfamiliar terrain and grow in your faith.

CULTIVATING SUPPORT and Accountability:

Join a Faith Community: Become part of a local church or faith community where you can connect with fellow believers. Attend services, join small groups, and participate in church events.

Build Close Relationships: Foster deep relationships with a few fellow believers who can walk with you closely on your discipleship journey. Share your struggles, pray together, and offer mutual support.

Mentorship: Seek out a mentor or spiritual leader who can provide guidance and accountability in your walk with God. Their wisdom and experience can be invaluable.

Participate in Small Groups: Many churches offer small groups or Bible studies where you can engage in discussions, study Scripture together, and receive support from peers.

Online Communities: If attending a physical church is challenging, consider joining online Christian communities or forums where you can connect with believers from around the world.

The Power of Support and Accountability:

Strength in Unity: Together, you and your fellow disciples form a unified body of believers, collectively seeking to follow Christ's teachings.

Shared Burdens: When you face challenges, the support of your faith community can help you carry the burden. Galatians 6:2 encourages believers to "bear one another's burdens."

Spiritual Growth: The accountability and encouragement provided by fellow believers contribute to your spiritual growth and maturity.

Prayer Support: Being part of a faith community means having a network of individuals who can pray for you and with you in times of need.

Community Witness: Your faith community becomes a witness to the world as you love and support one another. Jesus said, "By this all people will know that you are my disciples if you have love for one another" (John 13:35).

Empowerment: Support and accountability empower you to live out your faith with greater boldness and authenticity.

Incorporating support and accountability from fellow believers into your discipleship journey strengthens your faith and helps you live a life that reflects the teachings and love of Jesus Christ.

Learning and Growth:

In a faith community, you have the opportunity to learn from others, share experiences, and grow together in your understanding of God's Word.

THE BENEFITS OF LEARNING and Growth in a Faith Community:

Collective Knowledge: A faith community brings together individuals with diverse backgrounds and perspectives. This collective knowledge enriches your understanding of Scripture and deepens your faith.

Spiritual Mentoring: Within a faith community, you can find mentors and experienced believers who can guide your spiritual growth, answer questions, and provide valuable insights.

Discussions and Bible Studies: Participating in group discussions and Bible studies allows you to explore Scripture from different angles and gain new perspectives on its teachings.

Sharing Experiences: Fellow believers can share their own experiences of faith, offering practical examples of how to apply biblical principles in everyday life.

Accountability: Learning and growing together in a faith community provides built-in accountability as you encourage one another to live out your faith.

Ways to Foster Learning and Growth in a Faith Community:

Attend Worship Services: Regularly attend worship services where you can hear sermons, engage in corporate worship, and learn from the teaching of your church leaders.

Join Bible Studies: Participate in Bible studies or small groups within your faith community. These settings encourage open discussion and the exploration of God's Word.

Ask Questions: Don't hesitate to ask questions when you're unsure about a particular biblical concept or passage. Seek guidance from mentors or knowledgeable individuals in your faith community.

Share Your Insights: Share your own insights and experiences with others. Your unique perspective may benefit fellow believers and spark meaningful discussions.

Serve Together: Engaging in service projects or missions within your faith community can deepen your understanding of Christian values and the practical application of faith.

Read and Study Together: Encourage group or family Bible reading and study sessions. Sharing your thoughts and reflections can enhance your understanding and provide mutual encouragement.

THE POWER OF LEARNING and Growth in a Faith Community:

Deeper Understanding: Learning from others broadens your understanding of God's Word and helps you see its relevance in various life situations.

Spiritual Growth: Engaging in group learning and growth experiences within your faith community contributes to your spiritual growth and maturity.

Community Support: The relationships formed within your faith community offer support, encouragement, and a sense of belonging as you navigate your discipleship journey.

Application of Faith: Learning together encourages the practical application of your faith, allowing you to live out the teachings of Jesus more authentically.

Shared Blessings: As you learn and grow together, you share in the blessings of spiritual insight and transformation, enriching the entire faith community.

Learning and growing together in a faith community fosters a sense of unity and shared purpose among believers. It enables you to glean wisdom from one another, deepen your understanding of God's Word, and apply your faith to everyday life in a meaningful way.

Service and Outreach: Being part of a faith community enables you to engage in meaningful service and outreach efforts, putting your faith into action.

The Significance of Service and Outreach:

Living Out Your Faith: Service and outreach provide tangible ways to live out the teachings of Jesus. It's an expression of love, compassion, and obedience to His command to love your neighbor.

Meeting Needs: Through service, you could meet the physical, emotional, and spiritual needs of others, demonstrating God's love in practical ways.

Community Impact: Engaging in service and outreach efforts can have a positive impact on your local community, fostering goodwill and making a difference in the lives of those you serve.

Witness and Evangelism: Service and outreach serve as a powerful witness to your faith. Your actions can speak louder than words and create opportunities for evangelism and sharing the gospel.

WAYS TO ENGAGE IN SERVICE and Outreach Within Your Faith Community:

Participate in Outreach Programs: Join existing outreach programs or initiatives within your faith community. These efforts are often well-organized and provide opportunities to serve.

Identify Community Needs: Assess the specific needs of your local community and work with your faith community to develop targeted service projects or partnerships with local organizations.

Form Ministry Teams: Form ministry teams or committees dedicated to service and outreach. These groups can brainstorm ideas, plan events, and coordinate efforts.

Mobilize Volunteers: Encourage fellow believers to volunteer their time, talents, and resources for service projects. The collective effort of your faith community can make a significant impact.

Build Relationships: Service and outreach efforts should go beyond meeting immediate needs. Build relationships with those you serve, fostering a sense of community and ongoing support.

Pray for Guidance: Seek God's guidance through prayer as you discern where and how to serve. Pray for the hearts of those you reach out to and for opportunities to share the gospel.

The Power of Service and Outreach in a Faith Community:

Demonstrates God's Love: Service and outreach demonstrate God's love in action, revealing His character and compassion to those you serve.

Fulfills Jesus' Command: Serving others fulfills Jesus' command to love your neighbor as yourself (Matthew 22:39) and to go and make disciples (Matthew 28:19-20).

Strengthens Community: Engaging in service and outreach efforts strengthens the sense of community and unity within your faith community.

Impactful Witness: Your service and outreach become an impactful witness to your faith, drawing people to Christ through your actions.

Empowers Transformation: Through service, you have the power to transform lives, both in the community and within your faith community.

Personal Growth: Engaging in service and outreach opportunities can lead to personal growth, increased empathy, and a deeper understanding of the needs of others.

Service and outreach efforts within your faith community not only benefit those you serve but also provide a meaningful way to live out your faith, grow spiritually, and be a light in your community. They demonstrate the love of Christ in practical ways and contribute to the overall mission of making disciples and sharing the gospel.

WORSHIP AND FELLOWSHIP:

Gathering with fellow believers for worship and fellowship is a source of spiritual nourishment and joy. It reminds you that you are part of a larger family in Christ.

The Significance of Worship and Fellowship:

Spiritual Refreshment: Worship provides a time of spiritual refreshment, allowing you to draw near to God, express your gratitude, and experience His presence.

Community Bonding: Fellowship within your faith community fosters a sense of belonging and strengthens the bonds of friendship and support among believers.

Corporate Worship: Corporate worship brings believers together to collectively praise and glorify God. It magnifies His name and reinforces a spirit of unity.

Encouragement and Edification: Fellow believers can encourage and edify one another through shared worship experiences, prayer, and mutual support.

Engaging in Worship and Fellowship:

Regular Attendance: Prioritize regular attendance at worship services and fellowship events within your faith community. Consistency allows you to grow in your faith and build meaningful relationships.

Participate Actively: Engage actively in worship services by singing, praying, and attentively listening to the message. Participate in discussions and activities during fellowship gatherings.

Serve in Worship: Consider serving in various capacities during worship services, such as music ministry, ushering, or reading Scripture. Serving enhances your sense of belonging and contribution.

Hospitality: Extend hospitality by inviting newcomers and visitors to join your worship and fellowship gatherings. Try to welcome and connect with newcomers.

Pray for One Another: Pray for your fellow believers, lifting up their needs and concerns. Share your own prayer requests and be open to praying for others.

Small Groups: Participate in or lead small groups within your faith community. These smaller gatherings provide opportunities for deeper fellowship and discussion.

The Power of Worship and Fellowship:

Draws You Closer to God: Worship brings you into God's presence, allowing you to draw closer to Him and experience His love and grace.

Strengthens Faith: Fellowship with other believers strengthens your faith as you share in worship, prayer, and the study of God's Word.

Sense of Belonging: Worship and fellowship create a sense of belonging and community, reassuring you that you are part of the family of God.

Mutual Encouragement: Fellow believers can encourage and uplift you in times of joy and trial, providing a support system for your discipleship journey.

Corporate Praise: Corporate worship magnifies the praise and glory given to God, creating a powerful atmosphere of worship.

Joy and Celebration: Gathering with fellow believers often leads to joy and celebration as you celebrate God's goodness and blessings together.

Worship and fellowship within your faith community are essential components of your discipleship journey. They provide opportunities for spiritual nourishment, growth, and the building of meaningful relationships. Embrace these moments as precious opportunities to connect with God and fellow believers.

In this chapter, we have explored the foundational elements of discipleship: prayer, the Bible, and a faith community. These are the building blocks of your journey as a disciple of Jesus. Just as a strong foundation ensures the stability of a building, these foundations will support and sustain your growth as a follower of Christ. As you continue to deepen your understanding of prayer, Scripture, and community, you'll find yourself better equipped for the challenges and joys of the discipleship journey.

Chapter 3: Embracing the Teachings of Jesus

IN THIS CHAPTER, WE will delve into the heart of discipleship—following in the footsteps of Jesus by embracing His teachings. The Gospels are a treasure trove of wisdom and guidance, and by studying them, you can learn how to apply these teachings to your daily life.

Love as the Foundation

Jesus' central teaching is about love. In Matthew 22:37-39, He tells us to love God with all our hearts and love our neighbors as ourselves. This forms the foundation of Christian discipleship:

Love for God:

Discipleship begins with a deep and genuine love for God. This love compels you to seek Him, worship Him, and obey His commandments out of devotion, not mere obligation.

The Significance of Love for God:

Foundation of Discipleship: Love for God is the foundational motivation for discipleship. It is the driving force behind your commitment to follow Jesus and live according to His teachings.

Authentic Worship: When you love God, your worship becomes an authentic expression of your heart's affection and reverence. It is not driven by duty but by a genuine desire to draw near to Him.

Obedience as a Response: Obedience to God's commandments is not a burdensome duty but a loving response to His grace and goodness. It flows from a heart that desires to please and honor Him.

Sustaining Love: Love for God sustains you in times of challenge and testing. It keeps you anchored in your faith and committed to the journey of discipleship.

Nurturing Love for God:

Prayer and Reflection: Spend time in prayer and reflection, seeking to deepen your love for God. Communicate with Him honestly and open your heart to His presence.

Study His Word: Dive into the Bible to learn more about God's character, His love for you, and His redemptive plan. Meditate on passages that reveal His love and grace.

Cultivate Gratitude: Gratitude fosters love. Regularly express thankfulness to God for His blessings, salvation, and presence in your life.

Serve Others: Express your love for God by serving others. As Jesus taught, when you serve the least of these, you serve Him (Matthew 25:40).

Fellowship and Worship: Engage in fellowship with other believers and participate in corporate worship. These activities can reignite your love for God as you join with others in praise and adoration.

The Power of Love for God:

Transformative Power: Love for God has the power to transform your heart and character, making you more like Christ.

Motivation for Obedience: When you love God, obedience becomes a joyful response to His love, not a mere checklist of rules.

Deepened Relationship: Love for God deepens your relationship with Him, creating intimacy and trust.

Steadfastness in Trials: Love for God provides the strength to remain steadfast in your faith, even when facing trials and difficulties.

Source of Joy: Loving God brings a sense of joy and fulfillment as you experience His presence and favor.

Impact on Others: Your love for God can be a powerful witness to others, drawing them to a relationship with Him.

Remember that love for God is not something you generate on your own; it is a response to His unconditional love for you. Nurture and cultivate this love as you journey in discipleship, allowing it to be the driving force that propels you closer to God and empowers you to live out His teachings.

Love for Others: Jesus' command to love your neighbor is a call to selflessness and compassion. It means caring for the needs of those around you, even when it's inconvenient or challenging.

THE SIGNIFICANCE OF Love for Others:

Core Teaching of Jesus: Loving others is at the heart of Jesus' teachings. It encapsulates the essence of the Christian faith and discipleship.

Practical Expression of Faith: Your love for others is a tangible and practical expression of your faith. It demonstrates the transformative power of the gospel.

Building Community: Love for others fosters a sense of community and unity among believers. It creates an environment of care, support, and mutual edification.

Witness to the World: When you love others selflessly, it serves as a powerful witness to the world, drawing people to Christ through your actions.

Practicing Love for Others:

Empathy: Seek to understand the perspectives, feelings, and needs of others. Empathy is the foundation of compassionate love.

Serve with Humility: Approach acts of service with humility, considering the needs of others as more important than your own (Philippians 2:3-4).

Forgive Freely: Forgiveness is an expression of love. Release grudges and extend forgiveness to those who have wronged you.

Generosity: Share your resources, time, and talents with those in need. Generosity is a practical way to demonstrate love.

Kindness and Compassion: Practice kindness and compassion in your interactions with others, showing care and concern for their well-being.

Active Listening: Be an active listener when others share their joys, sorrows, and concerns. Give them your full attention and empathy.

The Power of Love for Others:

Demonstrates Christ's Love: Your love for others reflects the love of Christ, making His presence known in the world.

Transformation of Relationships: Love has the power to heal and transform broken relationships, fostering reconciliation and unity.

Impact on the Vulnerable: Your love can make a profound difference in the lives of the marginalized, oppressed, and vulnerable.

Unity in the Church: Love for others fosters unity and harmony within the church, creating a welcoming and supportive community.

Evangelistic Tool: Acts of love and compassion can open doors for sharing the gospel with those who may not have encountered it otherwise.

Personal Fulfillment: Loving others brings personal fulfillment and joy, as you experience the blessings of selflessness and sacrificial love.

AS A DISCIPLE OF JESUS, your love for others is a central aspect of your journey. It transforms your character, deepens your relationship with God, and impacts the world around you. Embrace the call to love your neighbor as yourself, allowing love for others to be a defining mark of your discipleship.

Forgiveness and Grace

One of the most powerful aspects of Jesus' teachings is forgiveness. He calls us to forgive as we have been forgiven. This means:

Extending Forgiveness: In discipleship, you'll encounter situations where forgiveness is difficult, but it's essential. Forgiving others frees you from the burden of bitterness and allows you to experience the peace that comes from God's forgiveness.

The Significance of Extending Forgiveness:

Following Jesus' Example: Forgiveness is at the core of Jesus' teachings. He modeled forgiveness on the cross, even while suffering unjustly.

Reconciliation: Forgiveness has the potential to restore broken relationships and foster reconciliation, reflecting the love and grace of God.

Inner Peace: Choosing to forgive releases you from the weight of anger and resentment, allowing you to experience inner peace and freedom.

Healing and Growth: Forgiveness can lead to healing and personal growth, both for the one who forgives and the one forgiven.

Practicing Forgiveness:

Acknowledge Hurt: Recognize the pain and hurt caused by the offense. It's important to acknowledge your emotions.

Choose Forgiveness: Forgiveness is a conscious choice. Decide to release the offender from the debt they owe you.

Pray for Help: Seek God's help in forgiving. Pray for the strength and grace to extend forgiveness, especially in challenging situations.

Let Go of Grudges: Release grudges and the desire for revenge. Choose to forgive and let go of the need for retaliation.

Boundaries: While forgiving, it's important to set healthy boundaries to protect yourself from further harm.

The Power of Extending Forgiveness:

Emotional Healing: Forgiveness can lead to emotional healing, allowing you to move forward without carrying the burden of anger or resentment.

Restored Relationships: Forgiveness has the potential to restore broken relationships and promote reconciliation.

Freedom from Bitterness: Extending forgiveness frees you from the bondage of bitterness, allowing you to experience joy and peace.

Spiritual Growth: Forgiveness is a mark of spiritual maturity, demonstrating your alignment with the teachings of Jesus.

Reflecting God's Love: Forgiveness reflects the love and grace of God, making His redemptive work visible in your life.

Witness to Others: Choosing to forgive can be a powerful witness to others, demonstrating the transformative power of Christ's love.

Remember that forgiveness does not always mean condoning the wrong or reconciling immediately. It means releasing the hold of bitterness and entrusting justice to God. In discipleship, forgiveness is an essential aspect of reflecting Christ's character and experiencing the healing and freedom He offers.

Receiving Forgiveness:

Recognizing your own need for forgiveness is humbling. Jesus teaches that God offers forgiveness to all who repent, providing a path to restoration.

The Significance of Receiving Forgiveness:

Acknowledging Imperfection: Receiving forgiveness acknowledges your imperfection and need for God's grace. It humbles you before Him.

Restoration and Healing: Forgiveness from God brings restoration and healing to your relationship with Him. It removes the barrier of sin.

Empathy and Compassion: Experiencing God's forgiveness deepens your empathy and compassion for others, as you recognize the same need in them.

Freedom from Guilt: Receiving forgiveness liberates you from guilt and shame, allowing you to walk in the freedom of God's grace.

Practicing Receiving Forgiveness:

Repentance: Repentance is a turning away from sin and a turning toward God. Acknowledge your sins, seek His forgiveness, and commit to change.

Confession: Confess your sins honestly and openly to God. He already knows your heart, but confession is an important step in receiving forgiveness.

Believe in God's Grace: Trust in God's promise of forgiveness through faith in Jesus Christ. Believe that His grace is sufficient to cover your sins.

Receive His Forgiveness: Embrace God's forgiveness as a gift. Know that your sins are forgiven and that you are reconciled to Him.

Walk in Repentance: After receiving forgiveness, live in a manner that reflects your gratitude and commitment to follow God's ways.

The Power of Receiving Forgiveness:

Restoration of Relationship: Receiving forgiveness restores your relationship with God, allowing you to draw near to Him.

Freedom from Guilt: God's forgiveness liberates you from the burden of guilt and shame, offering a sense of spiritual cleansing.

Empowerment for Change: Knowing that you are forgiven empowers you to make positive changes in your life and grow in your discipleship journey.

Reflecting God's Grace: Receiving forgiveness allows you to reflect God's grace to others, demonstrating His love and mercy.

Spiritual Renewal: The experience of forgiveness can lead to spiritual renewal, as you recommit to following God's path and living a life that pleases Him.

Witness to God's Love: Your own experience of receiving forgiveness can serve as a powerful witness to others, illustrating the transformative power of God's love.

Receiving forgiveness is an essential aspect of discipleship. It acknowledges your dependence on God's grace, humbles your heart, and empowers you to grow in your relationship with Him. It's a reminder that no one is beyond the reach of God's forgiveness and love.

Compassion and Service

Jesus' life was marked by compassion and service to others. He calls us to follow His example:

Compassion: Discipleship means opening your heart to the needs and suffering of others. Jesus showed compassion to the sick, the marginalized, and the outcasts, and He calls you to do the same.

The Significance of Compassion:

Imitating Christ: Compassion reflects Christ's character. It imitates His love and care for those who are hurting and in need.

Living Out the Gospel: Compassion is a practical way to live out the gospel message. It demonstrates God's love in action.

Building Relationships: Compassion fosters meaningful relationships with those you serve, allowing you to connect on a deeper level.

Bringing Hope: Your compassion can bring hope and relief to those facing difficult circumstances, reminding them of God's love.

Practicing Compassion:

Empathy: Cultivate empathy by seeking to understand the feelings and experiences of others. Put yourself in their shoes to better comprehend their struggles.

Acts of Kindness: Engage in acts of kindness, both big and small, to alleviate the suffering of others. Simple gestures can make a significant difference.

Listen and Care: Take the time to listen actively to people's stories and concerns. Show genuine care and concern for their well-being.

Serve the Vulnerable: Seek out opportunities to serve the vulnerable and marginalized in your community. This can include volunteering at shelters, food banks, or outreach programs.

Prayer: Pray for those who are suffering or in need. Lift their burdens to God and intercede on their behalf.

Advocacy: Speak up for those who cannot advocate for themselves. Be a voice for justice and mercy in your community and beyond.

The Power of Compassion:

Reflecting Christ's Heart: Compassion reflects the heart of Christ, who came to seek and save the lost (Luke 19:10) and bind up the brokenhearted (Isaiah 61:1).

Transformative Impact: Compassion has the power to transform lives and communities. It can provide a lifeline of hope to those facing despair.

Unity in the Church: Compassion fosters unity within the church as believers come together to serve and care for one another and their community.

Witness to the World: Your acts of compassion serve as a powerful witness to the world, demonstrating the love and mercy of Christ.

Personal Growth: Engaging in compassionate acts deepens your own faith and character, making you more Christlike.

Bringing Glory to God: Ultimately, your compassion brings glory to God as you reflect His love and compassion to a hurting world.

Compassion is not only a vital aspect of discipleship but also a reflection of God's heart for His creation. As you open your heart to the needs and suffering of others, you participate in the redemptive work of Christ and bring hope to a broken world.

SERVICE: Serving others is a tangible expression of your faith. Whether through acts of kindness, generosity, or volunteering, disciples are called to serve those in need.

The Significance of Service:

Following Jesus' Example: Jesus exemplified servanthood throughout His ministry, teaching His disciples to serve one another and the world.

Living Out the Gospel: Service is a practical way to live out the gospel message. It demonstrates God's love and the selflessness of the Christian faith.

Building Relationships: Through service, you build meaningful relationships with those you serve, fostering a sense of community and unity.

Witness to Others: Service serves as a powerful witness to others, drawing people to Christ through your actions.

Practicing Service:

Identify Needs: Be attentive to the needs of those around you, both in your faith community and in your wider community. Seek out opportunities to serve.

Acts of Kindness: Engage in everyday acts of kindness, such as helping a neighbor, offering assistance to someone in need, or showing generosity to those less fortunate.

Volunteering: Dedicate your time and skills to volunteer for organizations, causes, or projects that align with your values and provide service to others.

Support and Encouragement: Offer support and encouragement to those facing difficult circumstances, whether through a listening ear, a helping hand, or a word of comfort.

Mentoring and Discipleship: Mentor and disciple others in their faith journey, sharing your knowledge and experiences to help them grow in their relationship with God.

Prayer and Intercession: Pray for those in need and intercede on their behalf. Prayer is a powerful form of service that can bring comfort and healing.

The Power of Service:

Reflecting Christ's Character: Service reflects the character of Christ, who came not to be served but to serve (Mark 10:45).

Transforming Lives: Service has the power to transform lives and communities, bringing positive change and hope.

Unity in the Church: Service fosters unity within the church as believers come together to serve one another and their community.

Witness to the World: Acts of service serve as a powerful witness to the world, demonstrating the love and compassion of Christ.

Personal Growth: Engaging in acts of service deepens your own faith and character, making you more Christlike.

Bringing Glory to God: Ultimately, service brings glory to God as you reflect His love and compassion to a hurting world.

Service is not only an essential aspect of discipleship but also a reflection of God's heart for His creation. As you serve others in various ways, you participate in the redemptive work of Christ and bring hope, healing, and love to a broken world.

The Sermon on the Mount

In Matthew 5-7, Jesus delivers the Sermon on the Mount, which contains some of His most profound teachings. It covers topics such as humility, peacemaking, purity of heart, and the importance of seeking God's kingdom above all else. This sermon provides a roadmap for living a life that aligns with God's kingdom values.

The Significance of the Sermon on the Mount:

Foundation of Christian Ethics: The Sermon on the Mount serves as a foundational guide for Christian ethics and morality. It outlines the principles by which disciples of Jesus should live.

Kingdom Values: Jesus presents the values and principles of God's kingdom, which often contrast with the values of the world. It challenges believers to live counter-culturally.

Transformation of Heart: The sermon emphasizes the transformation of the heart and inner character rather than mere external actions. It addresses the root causes of sinful behavior.

Call to Discipleship: The teachings in this sermon lay out a clear call to discipleship, inviting believers to follow Jesus in a radical and wholehearted way.

Key Teachings from the Sermon on the Mount:

1. **The Beatitudes (Matthew 5:3-12):** These describe the characteristics and blessings of those in God's kingdom, including the meek, the merciful, and the peacemakers.
2. **Salt and Light (Matthew 5:13-16):** Believers are called to be salt and light in the world, influencing it positively and shining God's truth and love.
3. **Fulfilling the Law (Matthew 5:17-48):** Jesus emphasizes the importance of fulfilling God's law not only externally but also internally, addressing issues such as anger, lust, and love for

enemies.

4. **The Lord's Prayer (Matthew 6:9-13):** Jesus provides a model prayer that emphasizes God's sovereignty, provision, and forgiveness.

5. **Seek First the Kingdom (Matthew 6:25-34):** Disciples are urged to prioritize seeking God's kingdom above material concerns, trusting in His provision.

6. **Judging Others (Matthew 7:1-6):** Believers are cautioned against hypocritical judgment and encouraged to address their own faults before helping others.

7. **The Golden Rule (Matthew 7:12):** The principle of treating others as you would want to be treated is a fundamental guide for ethical living.

8. **The Narrow and Wide Gates (Matthew 7:13-14):** Jesus calls for a narrow and challenging path that leads to life, in contrast to the broad way that leads to destruction.

Application in Discipleship:

Heart Transformation: The Sermon on the Mount challenges believers to allow Jesus to transform their hearts and character. It calls for an authentic, inward faith that reflects outwardly.

Living Counter-Culturally: Disciples are encouraged to live in a way that stands out from the values and priorities of the world, demonstrating a commitment to God's kingdom.

Prioritizing Prayer: The Lord's Prayer offers a model for effective prayer, emphasizing God's lordship, provision, and forgiveness.

Humility and Peacemaking: Disciples are called to embrace humility, practice peacemaking, and exhibit Christlike virtues in their interactions with others.

Seeking God's Kingdom: The teaching to seek first God's kingdom challenges disciples to prioritize their relationship with God above all else.

Non-Judgmental Attitude: Believers are encouraged to adopt a non-judgmental attitude while addressing their own shortcomings and extending grace to others.

The Sermon on the Mount is a treasure trove of spiritual wisdom and guidance for discipleship. It offers a roadmap for living a life that aligns with God's kingdom values and exemplifies the character of Christ.

PRAYER AND TRUST

Throughout the Gospels, Jesus emphasizes the importance of prayer and trust in God:

Prayer: Jesus often withdrew to pray, showing the necessity of connecting with God through prayer. Prayer is your lifeline to God, where you seek His guidance, find strength, and express your trust in Him.

The Significance of Prayer:

1. **Communion with God:** Prayer is a means of communion and relationship with God. It allows you to draw near to Him, sharing your thoughts, concerns, and desires.
2. **Guidance and Direction:** Through prayer, you seek God's guidance and wisdom for life's decisions and challenges. It aligns your will with His.
3. **Strength and Comfort:** Prayer provides strength and comfort in times of difficulty, allowing you to cast your cares upon God and find solace in His presence.

4. **Expression of Trust:** Prayer is an expression of trust in God's providence and sovereignty over all aspects of life.

Practicing Prayer:

Regular Devotion: Establish a regular pattern of prayer in your daily life. Dedicate specific times for focused prayer and communion with God.

Variety of Prayer: Engage in different forms of prayer, including intercession for others, thanksgiving, confession, and adoration.

Listening: Prayer is not only about speaking but also about listening. Take time to listen to God's voice through His Word and in moments of silence.

Pray without Ceasing: Cultivate an ongoing conversation with God throughout your day, seeking His guidance and acknowledging His presence in all you do.

Pray in Faith: Approach God in faith, believing that He hears and answers your prayers according to His will.

Persistence: Be persistent in prayer, especially when facing challenges or waiting for answers. Jesus encourages persistence in prayer (Luke 18:1-8).

The Power of Prayer:

1. **Spiritual Growth:** Prayer deepens your spiritual life, fostering intimacy with God and strengthening your faith.
2. **Guidance and Clarity:** Prayer provides guidance and clarity in decision-making, helping you align your choices with God's will.
3. **Peace and Comfort:** In times of trouble, prayer offers peace and comfort as you entrust your concerns to God.
4. **Empowerment for Service:** Prayer empowers you for service

and equips you with the strength to carry out God's work.

5. **Connection with Others:** Through intercessory prayer, you connect with and support others in their journeys of faith.

6. **Witness to Others:** Your commitment to prayer can be a powerful witness to others, illustrating your dependence on God and His transformative work in your life.

Prayer is a vital component of discipleship, allowing you to draw near to God, seek His guidance, and find strength and comfort in His presence. It is a means of deepening your relationship with Him and aligning your life with His purposes.

Trust: Discipleship involves trusting God's plan, even when circumstances are challenging. Jesus' own trust in God was unwavering, and He encourages you to have faith and trust in God's goodness.

The Significance of Trust:

Foundation of Faith: Trust is the foundation of your faith in God. It involves believing in His character, sovereignty, and faithfulness.

Surrender to God: Trust requires surrendering control and acknowledging that God's plans are higher and wiser than your own.

Peace in Uncertainty: Trusting God provides peace and assurance, even during uncertainty and adversity.

Faith in Action: Trust is not merely a passive belief but an active commitment to live in accordance with God's promises and guidance.

Practicing Trust:

Seek God's Guidance: Trust involves seeking God's guidance in decision-making, acknowledging His wisdom and understanding surpass your own.

Reflect on His Faithfulness: Remind yourself of times when God has been faithful in your life or in the lives of others. This strengthens your trust.

Prayer and Surrender: In prayer, express your trust in God's plan and surrender your concerns to Him. Let go of anxieties and rest in His care.

Stay in His Word: Regularly read and meditate on God's Word to deepen your understanding of His character and promises.

Community Support: Engage with a faith community that encourages and strengthens your trust in God.

The Power of Trust:

Strengthened Faith: Trusting God strengthens your faith and reliance on Him, deepening your relationship with Him.

Peace in Trials: Trust provides peace and stability, allowing you to navigate trials and challenges with confidence.

Guidance and Direction: Trusting God's guidance leads to wise decisions and a life aligned with His purposes.

Empowerment for Obedience: Trust enables you to obey God's commands and follow His teachings, even when they are countercultural or challenging.

Witness to Others: Your trust in God's faithfulness and goodness can serve as a powerful witness to those around you.

Restoration and Healing: Trusting God in times of brokenness or pain can lead to restoration and healing as you rely on His grace and provision.

Jesus exemplified unwavering trust in God throughout His life and ministry, even in the face of suffering and death. As His disciple, you are called to emulate this trust, believing in God's goodness, sovereignty, and faithfulness. Trust is a cornerstone of your discipleship journey, allowing you to walk in faith and confidence.

In this chapter, we have explored the teachings of Jesus found in the Gospels. These teachings are the blueprint for living a life of discipleship. By embracing love, forgiveness, compassion, and other core principles, you can walk in the footsteps of Jesus and grow into a disciple who reflects His character and teachings in your daily life.

Remember that discipleship is not just about knowing these teachings but also living them out authentically, with a heart transformed by the grace of Christ.

Chapter 4: The Power of Grace

GRACE IS THE UNMERITED favor and love of God, and it is at the heart of the Christian faith. In this chapter, we will delve into the concept of grace and its transformative power in the life of a disciple.

Understanding Grace

Grace is a fundamental concept in the Christian faith, and it plays a central role in discipleship. Understanding grace is essential for every believer as it profoundly shapes your relationship with God and your journey as a disciple of Jesus.

The Significance of Grace:

Unmerited Favor: Grace is God's unmerited favor and love extended to humanity. It's a gift you receive despite your unworthiness.

Salvation: Grace is the means through which God offers salvation to humanity. It's the undeserved forgiveness and reconciliation made possible through Jesus Christ.

Transformation: Grace not only saves but also transforms. It empowers you to live a righteous and Christlike life as you grow in your discipleship.

Freedom from Guilt: Grace offers freedom from guilt and shame, reminding you that your sins are forgiven through faith in Christ.

PRACTICING GRACE:

1. **Receive God's Gift:** Embrace God's grace as a free gift.

Understand that your salvation is not based on your works but on God's love and mercy.

2. **Extend Grace to Others:** Just as you have received grace, extend grace to others. Forgive and show compassion as God has shown to you.

3. **Live a Transformed Life:** Allow God's grace to transform your character and behavior. Seek to live a life that reflects the grace you've received.

4. **Daily Dependence:** Recognize your daily need for God's grace. Approach each day with humility, acknowledging your dependence on Him.

5. **Gratitude:** Cultivate a heart of gratitude for God's grace. Thank Him for His love and forgiveness.

The Power of Grace:

Salvation: Grace is the foundation of your salvation, as it is through God's grace that you are justified and reconciled to Him.

Transformation: Grace empowers you to overcome sin and grow in holiness. It molds you into the image of Christ.

Freedom: Grace liberates you from the bondage of legalism and self-righteousness. It frees you to live in the joy of God's acceptance.

Assurance: Grace provides assurance of God's love and forgiveness, erasing doubt and fear.

Empathy: Experiencing God's grace enables you to show empathy and compassion to others who are in need of grace.

Witness: Your life, shaped by grace, becomes a powerful witness to God's love and mercy.

Understanding grace is not only a foundational aspect of discipleship but also a continual journey of discovery. As you grasp the depth of God's grace, you will experience its transforming power in your life, shaping you into a faithful and joyful disciple of Jesus.

Unearned and Undeserved: Grace is a gift from God that we do not earn or deserve. It is freely given because of God's boundless love and mercy. As a disciple, you are a recipient of this amazing grace.

The Significance of Unearned and Undeserved Grace:

1. **Humility:** Recognizing that grace is unearned and undeserved humbles the believer, acknowledging their reliance on God's mercy.
2. **Thanksgiving:** Unearned grace inspires gratitude and thanksgiving to God for His lavish love and forgiveness.
3. **Freedom:** Understanding grace as unearned and undeserved liberates believers from the burden of striving to earn salvation through their own efforts.
4. **Motivation for Obedience:** Grace motivates believers to obey and serve God out of love and gratitude rather than a sense of obligation.

PRACTICING UNEARNED and Undeserved Grace:

Embrace Humility: Embrace humility in recognizing that your salvation and God's blessings are gifts you did not earn or deserve.

Express Gratitude: Continually express gratitude to God for His unearned and undeserved grace in your life.

Extend Grace to Others: As you have received grace, extend grace to others, showing love, forgiveness, and compassion.

Live with Freedom: Live in the freedom that comes from knowing your acceptance by God is not based on your performance.

The Power of Unearned and Undeserved Grace:

Salvation: Unearned and undeserved grace is the foundation of salvation, offering forgiveness and reconciliation to all who believe.

Freedom from Legalism: Understanding grace liberates believers from legalism and self-righteousness, allowing them to rest in God's love.

Transformed Hearts: The awareness of unearned grace transforms hearts, motivating believers to live in accordance with God's will.

Witness to God's Love: Living as recipients of unearned grace becomes a powerful witness to the world of God's love and mercy.

Motivation for Service: Unearned grace motivates believers to serve and obey God out of love and devotion rather than fear or duty.

Unearned and undeserved grace is a foundational concept in Christianity, underscoring God's unfathomable love and the essence of discipleship. As you grasp the depth of this grace, it becomes a wellspring of joy, humility, and motivation in your journey as a disciple of Jesus.

The Role of Grace in Salvation: Grace is the foundation of your salvation. Ephesians 2:8-9 reminds us that "For by grace you have been saved through faith. And this is not your own doing; it is the gift of God, not a result of works so that no one may boast." Your salvation is a result of God's grace, not your own efforts.

The Significance of Grace in Salvation:

1. **Gift of God:** Salvation is a gift from God, made possible by

His grace. It cannot be earned through good deeds or human merit.

2. **Humility:** Recognizing that salvation is entirely a product of God's grace fosters humility, as it underscores your dependence on Him for redemption.

3. **Freedom from Boasting:** Grace in salvation eliminates boasting, as no one can claim to have earned their salvation. It places the focus on God's goodness and love.

PRACTICING THE ROLE of Grace in Salvation:

Receive the Gift: Acknowledge and receive salvation as a gift of God's grace, understanding that you cannot earn it through your own efforts.

Express Gratitude: Continually express gratitude to God for His grace in providing salvation through Jesus Christ.

Share the Good News: Share the message of salvation by grace through faith with others, emphasizing that it is a gift available to all who believe.

Walk in Humility: Live in humility, recognizing that your salvation is solely a result of God's grace and not your own righteousness.

The Power of Grace in Salvation:

Redemption: Grace in salvation provides the means of redemption and reconciliation with God for all who believe.

Assurance: Understanding grace in salvation offers assurance, as believers trust in the sufficiency of Christ's work on the cross.

Freedom: Grace liberates individuals from the burden of striving to earn salvation and allows them to rest in God's unmerited favor.

Unity in Christ: Grace in salvation unites believers of diverse backgrounds, as all are saved by the same grace through faith in Jesus.

Motivation for Service: Salvation by grace motivates believers to serve and obey God out of love and gratitude rather than a sense of obligation.

The role of grace in salvation is a foundational truth in Christianity, emphasizing God's unmerited favor and the work of Christ on the cross. It is a reminder that salvation is a gift, not an achievement, and it humbles the believer while inspiring gratitude and a deep love for God. Understanding this role of grace is essential for every disciple of Jesus.

Repentance and Forgiveness

Repentance and forgiveness are pivotal aspects of the Christian faith and discipleship. They are inseparable from the concept of grace and play a central role in your relationship with God and your journey as a disciple of Jesus.

The Significance of Repentance and Forgiveness:

1. **Turning Towards God:** Repentance involves a turning away from sin and a turning toward God. It's a change of heart and mind that leads to a renewed relationship with Him.
2. **Restoration:** Repentance and forgiveness lead to spiritual restoration and reconciliation with God. They mend the brokenness caused by sin.
3. **Freedom from Guilt:** Forgiveness releases believers from the burden of guilt and shame, reminding them of God's gracious offer of mercy and pardon.
4. **Holiness:** Repentance and forgiveness are integral to the process of becoming more Christlike and living a life of holiness.

Practicing Repentance and Forgiveness:

Recognize Sin: Acknowledge and take responsibility for your sins, confessing them to God in prayer.

Sincere Contrition: Approach repentance with sincere contrition and a genuine desire to turn away from sin.

Seek God's Forgiveness: Seek God's forgiveness with a repentant heart, knowing that He is faithful to forgive (1 John 1:9).

Extend Forgiveness: Just as you seek forgiveness from God, extend forgiveness to others who have wronged you.

Repentance as a Lifestyle: Make repentance a lifestyle by continually examining your heart and actions in light of God's Word.

The Power of Repentance and Forgiveness:

Reconciliation with God: Repentance and forgiveness facilitate reconciliation with God, mending the relationship damaged by sin.

Freedom from Bondage: Forgiveness frees believers from the bondage of sin, allowing them to live in the liberty of God's grace.

Restoration of Joy: As believers experience forgiveness, they often find a restoration of joy and peace in their relationship with God.

Transformation: Repentance and forgiveness are catalysts for personal transformation, leading to a more Christlike character.

Witness to God's Grace: A life marked by repentance and forgiveness serves as a powerful witness to the transformative power of God's grace.

Unity in the Church: Practicing forgiveness within the faith community promotes unity and reconciliation among believers.

Repentance and forgiveness are not one-time events but ongoing processes in the life of a disciple. They reflect the heart of God, who extends His grace and mercy to all who turn to Him in repentance. Embracing and practicing these principles are essential for spiritual growth and a vibrant discipleship journey.

The Call to Repentance: Discipleship involves recognizing your need for God's grace and forgiveness. This begins with repentance—an honest acknowledgment of your sins and a turning away from them. Acts 3:19 tells us to "Repent, then, and turn to God, so that your sins may be wiped out."

The Significance of the Call to Repentance:

Recognition of Sin: Repentance requires recognizing your sins and their separation from God's holiness.

Turning Toward God: Repentance is a turning away from sin and a turning toward God. It signifies a change of heart and a desire for a renewed relationship with Him.

Preparation for Forgiveness: Repentance prepares the heart for God's forgiveness and the cleansing of sin.

Lifestyle of Discipleship: Repentance is not a one-time event but a continual aspect of a disciple's life, as it involves ongoing spiritual growth and transformation.

Practicing the Call to Repentance:

Examination of Conscience: Regularly examine your thoughts, actions, and attitudes in light of God's Word to identify areas that need repentance.

Confession to God: Confess your sins honestly to God in prayer, acknowledging your need for His forgiveness.

Sincere Contrition: Approach repentance with sincere contrition and a genuine desire to turn away from sin.

Receive God's Forgiveness: Trust in God's promise of forgiveness and the cleansing of sin through Jesus Christ.

Spiritual Accountability: Seek accountability and support from fellow believers to help you in your journey of repentance and discipleship.

The Power of the Call to Repentance:

1. **Reconciliation with God:** Repentance leads to reconciliation with God, restoring the broken relationship caused by sin.
2. **Freedom from Guilt:** It offers freedom from guilt and shame, reminding believers of God's gracious offer of mercy and pardon.
3. **Holiness:** Repentance is integral to the process of becoming more Christlike and living a life of holiness.
4. **Restoration of Joy:** Believers often find a restoration of joy and peace in their relationship with God as they experience His forgiveness.
5. **Witness to God's Grace:** A life marked by repentance serves as a powerful witness to the transformative power of God's grace.
6. **Continual Growth:** Repentance is a catalyst for personal transformation, leading to spiritual growth and maturity.

The call to repentance is an essential component of discipleship, prompting believers to continually turn toward God, acknowledge their need for His grace, and experience the transformation that comes from a life of repentance and forgiveness.

God's Forgiveness: The beauty of God's grace is seen in His willingness to forgive. 1 John 1:9 assures us that "If we confess our sins, He is faithful and just to forgive us our sins and to cleanse us from all unrighteousness." God's forgiveness is not only a pardon but also a cleansing that allows you to start anew.

The Significance of God's Forgiveness:

Pardon: God's forgiveness is a complete pardon of your sins, removing the guilt and consequences of wrongdoing.

Cleansing: It includes cleansing from all unrighteousness, purifying the heart and renewing your relationship with God.

Restoration: God's forgiveness leads to the restoration of your fellowship with Him, mending the brokenness caused by sin.

Assurance: The assurance of God's forgiveness provides peace and confidence in your relationship with Him.

Practicing God's Forgiveness:

Confession: Confess your sins honestly and specifically to God, acknowledging your need for His forgiveness.

Trust in God's Faithfulness: Trust in God's faithfulness and justice to forgive your sins when you confess them.

Accept His Forgiveness: Accept God's forgiveness with gratitude and a heart willing to turn away from sin.

Forgive Others: Extend the forgiveness you have received from God to others who have wronged you.

Live in Freedom: Live in the freedom of God's forgiveness, knowing that you are no longer held captive by guilt and shame.

The Power of God's Forgiveness:

Reconciliation: God's forgiveness facilitates reconciliation with Him, restoring the broken relationship caused by sin.

Freedom from Guilt: It offers freedom from the burden of guilt and shame, reminding believers of God's gracious offer of mercy and pardon.

Spiritual Renewal: God's forgiveness includes cleansing, resulting in spiritual renewal and a transformed heart.

Assurance: Believers can have assurance of their forgiveness, knowing that God is faithful to His promise.

Witness to God's Love: Experiencing and extending God's forgiveness becomes a powerful witness to the world of His love and mercy.

Motivation for Obedience: God's forgiveness motivates believers to obey and serve Him out of love and gratitude.

God's forgiveness is a cornerstone of the Christian faith and discipleship. It reflects His boundless love, grace, and desire for restored fellowship with His children. Embracing and practicing God's forgiveness is essential for spiritual growth and a vibrant discipleship journey.

The Transformational Power of God's Love

God's love is a powerful force that has the capacity to transform the lives of those who embrace it. In discipleship, understanding and experiencing God's love is central to personal growth and becoming more Christlike.

The Significance of God's Love:

1. **Unconditional:** God's love is unconditional and not based on human merit or performance. It is freely given to all who believe.
2. **Transformative:** His love has the power to transform hearts, renew minds, and change lives from the inside out.
3. **Motivating:** God's love motivates believers to love Him in return and to love others as He has loved them.
4. **Assurance:** It offers assurance of God's presence, care, and faithfulness, even during challenges.

Practicing the Transformational Power of God's Love:

Receive God's Love: Embrace God's love as a personal reality. Believe that you are deeply loved by Him.

Reflect on His Love: Regularly meditate on God's love, using Scriptures that emphasize His love for you.

Extend Love to Others: Practice loving others unconditionally, just as God loves you.

Forgive and Show Compassion: Show forgiveness and compassion to those who wrong you, reflecting God's love in your relationships.

Serve with Love: Serve others with love and humility, recognizing that God's love compels you to be a servant to all.

The Power of God's Love:

Transformation: God's love transforms hearts, leading to a renewed mind and a Christlike character.

Healing: His love brings healing and restoration to wounded souls, offering comfort and hope.

Motivation for Obedience: Believers are motivated to obey God's commandments out of love for Him.

Unity: God's love fosters unity among believers, breaking down barriers and promoting harmony.

Witness to the World: A community marked by God's love serves as a powerful witness to the world, drawing others to Christ.

Sustaining in Trials: God's love sustains and comforts believers in times of trial and suffering.

Understanding and embracing God's love is a lifelong journey in discipleship. As you immerse yourself in His love, you will experience personal transformation, a deepened relationship with God, and a compelling love for others. God's love is the wellspring of your discipleship journey, providing strength, motivation, and the power to become more like Jesus.

Inner Transformation: Grace not only forgives but also transforms. As a disciple, you experience an inner transformation as you encounter God's love. Romans 12:2 encourages you to "be transformed by the renewing of your mind." This renewal is a result of God's grace at work within you.

The Significance of Inner Transformation:

Renewed Mind: Inner transformation involves the renewal of your mind, aligning your thoughts and attitudes with God's truth and love.

Character Change: It leads to a transformation of character, producing the fruit of the Spirit, such as love, joy, peace, patience, and kindness.

Spiritual Growth: Inner transformation fosters spiritual growth, enabling you to become more Christlike in your actions and responses.

Reflecting God's Image: As you are transformed from the inside out, you increasingly reflect the image of God in your life.

PRACTICING INNER TRANSFORMATION:

Engage in Spiritual Disciplines: Regularly engage in spiritual disciplines such as prayer, Bible study, meditation, and worship to cultivate inner transformation.

Surrender to God's Work: Surrender to the work of the Holy Spirit within you, allowing Him to convict, guide, and transform your heart.

Renew Your Mind: Meditate on God's Word and replace negative or ungodly thought patterns with biblical truths.

Reflect on God's Love: Continually reflect on God's love for you and allow His love to motivate and shape your actions.

Practice Obedience: Obedience to God's Word and His leading is a practical way to experience inner transformation.

The Power of Inner Transformation:

1. **Christlikeness:** Inner transformation results in a life that increasingly reflects the character and nature of Christ.

2. **Fruit of the Spirit:** It produces the fruit of the Spirit, which is evidence of God's work within you.

3. **Spiritual Maturity:** Inner transformation leads to spiritual maturity, enabling you to navigate life's challenges with wisdom and grace.

4. **Witness to God's Grace:** Your transformed life becomes a powerful witness to the transformative power of God's grace.

5. **Alignment with God's Will:** Inner transformation aligns your desires and choices with God's will, leading to a more purposeful and fulfilling life.

6. **Impact on Others:** As you are transformed, you have a positive impact on those around you, inspiring others to seek God's transformative love.

Inner transformation is a hallmark of discipleship, and it reflects God's ongoing work in the lives of His children. As you open yourself to His transformative love, your inner being is renewed, and you become a living testimony to the power of His grace.

Empowerment for Change: Grace empowers you to live a life that honors God. Titus 2:11-12 explains that "For the grace of God has appeared, bringing salvation for all people, training us to renounce ungodliness and worldly passions, and to live self-controlled, upright, and godly lives." God's grace trains and equips you to live in a way that reflects His character.

The Significance of Empowerment for Change:

Transformation: Grace empowers you to renounce ungodliness and embrace a life characterized by godliness and righteousness.

Training: It serves as a training ground for discipleship, teaching you to live self-controlled and upright lives.

Alignment with God's Will: Empowerment for change aligns your desires and actions with God's will, enabling you to walk in obedience.

Holiness: Grace empowers you to pursue holiness and a life that reflects the holiness of God.

Practicing Empowerment for Change:

1. **Embrace God's Grace:** Embrace the empowerment of God's grace by acknowledging your need for it in your daily life.
2. **Renounce Ungodliness:** Identify areas of ungodliness and sin in your life, and with the help of God's grace, take steps to renounce and turn away from them.
3. **Cultivate Self-Control:** Practice self-control in your thoughts, actions, and responses, relying on God's grace to strengthen you.
4. **Pursue Godliness:** Make the pursuit of godliness a priority, seeking to grow in Christlikeness through the power of grace.
5. **Obedience to God's Word:** Obey God's Word and His leading, allowing grace to empower you in living a life that aligns with His commands.

The Power of Empowerment for Change:

Holiness: Empowerment for change leads to a life of holiness and conformity to God's character.

Victory Over Sin: Grace empowers you to gain victory over sin and worldly passions.

Fruitful Discipleship: It enables you to bear the fruit of godliness and righteousness in your life.

Effective Witness: A life empowered by grace serves as a powerful witness to the transformative work of God.

Freedom: Grace liberates you from the bondage of sin, enabling you to live in the freedom of God's love and acceptance.

Growth in Discipleship: Empowerment for change fosters continual growth and maturation in your discipleship journey.

God's grace not only forgives sins but also empowers you to live a life that reflects His love, holiness, and righteousness. As you yield to the empowering work of grace, you will experience transformation and become a more effective disciple of Jesus.

Extending Grace to Others

As a disciple of Jesus, extending grace to others is a fundamental aspect of living out your faith. Just as you have received God's grace, you are called to show grace and kindness to those around you.

The Significance of Extending Grace to Others:

1. **Imitating Christ:** Extending grace reflects the character of Christ, who showed grace and compassion to all.
2. **Forgiveness:** It promotes forgiveness and reconciliation in relationships, fostering peace and unity.
3. **Witness to God's Love:** Extending grace becomes a powerful witness to God's love and mercy in action.
4. **Reflecting God's Heart:** It reflects God's heart for humanity, as He desires all to experience His grace and salvation.

Practicing Extending Grace to Others:

Forgive Freely: Forgive others as you have been forgiven by God, releasing any grudges or bitterness.

Show Kindness: Extend acts of kindness and compassion to those in need, demonstrating God's love.

Be Patient: Practice patience and understanding in your interactions, giving others room to grow and change.

Listen and Empathize: Listen actively to others and empathize with their struggles and challenges.

Offer Encouragement: Encourage and uplift those who are discouraged or facing difficulties.

Seek Reconciliation: If conflicts arise, seek reconciliation and restoration in relationships.

The Power of Extending Grace to Others:

1. **Healing Relationships:** Extending grace promotes healing in broken relationships, fostering reconciliation.
2. **Transformation:** It has the potential to transform lives as people experience God's love through your actions.
3. **Unity in the Church:** Grace strengthens unity and harmony within the faith community.
4. **Effective Witness:** A community marked by grace becomes an effective witness to the world.
5. **Growth in Love:** Extending grace deepens your love for others and helps you grow in Christlikeness.
6. **Reflecting God's Heart:** It reflects God's heart for humanity, as He desires all to experience His grace and salvation.

Extending grace to others is not always easy, but it is a central aspect of discipleship. It requires humility, compassion, and a heart that reflects the love of Christ. As you practice extending grace, you become a channel of God's love and a source of hope and healing to those around you.

Forgiving Others: Just as you receive God's grace and forgiveness, you are called to extend the same to others. In Matthew 6:14-15, Jesus emphasizes the importance of forgiving others: "For if you forgive others their trespasses, your heavenly Father will also forgive you, but if you do not forgive others their trespasses, neither will your Father forgive your trespasses."

The Significance of Forgiving Others:

Reflection of God's Grace: Forgiving others reflects the grace and forgiveness you have received from God.

Obedience to Christ: It is an act of obedience to Christ's teachings, as He emphasizes the importance of forgiveness.

Healing in Relationships: Forgiveness promotes healing and reconciliation in broken relationships.

Freedom from Bitterness: Forgiving others releases you from the burden of bitterness and resentment.

Practicing Forgiving Others:

1. **Acknowledge the Hurt:** Recognize the hurt or offense caused by others, acknowledging your feelings.
2. **Choose Forgiveness:** Make a conscious decision to forgive, choosing to release the debt owed to you.
3. **Pray for Those Who Hurt You:** Pray for the individuals who have wronged you, asking God to bless them and bring healing to their lives.
4. **Let Go of Resentment:** Release any lingering resentment or anger, choosing to replace them with love and compassion.
5. **Seek Reconciliation:** If appropriate and possible, seek reconciliation and restoration in the relationship.
6. **Set Boundaries:** In cases where reconciliation may not be possible or safe, set healthy boundaries to protect yourself.

The Power of Forgiving Others:

Healing Relationships: Forgiveness promotes healing and reconciliation in broken relationships.

Freedom from Bitterness: It releases you from the burden of bitterness and resentment, allowing you to experience freedom and peace.

Spiritual Growth: Forgiving others is a catalyst for personal spiritual growth and maturity.

Reflecting God's Love: It reflects God's love and grace in action, serving as a witness to His transformative power.

Unity in the Church: Forgiving others fosters unity and harmony within the faith community.

Obedience to Christ: Forgiving others is an act of obedience to Christ's commandments.

Forgiving others can be challenging, especially in cases of deep hurt or betrayal. However, it is an essential aspect of discipleship that aligns with God's heart for reconciliation and restoration. As you practice forgiveness, you mirror God's grace and become an instrument of healing and hope in the lives of others.

Showing Compassion: Grace also compels you to show compassion and love to those who have wronged you. Romans 12:20 reminds you to "if your enemy is hungry, feed him; if he is thirsty, give him something to drink."

The Significance of Showing Compassion:

1. **Demonstrates Christlike Love:** Showing compassion reflects the love and mercy of Christ, who showed compassion even to those who opposed Him.

2. **Breaks the Cycle of Hostility:** Compassion has the power to break the cycle of hostility and retaliation, fostering an atmosphere of peace.
3. **Witness to God's Love:** It serves as a powerful witness to God's love and transformative work in your life.
4. **Opportunity for Redemption:** Compassion offers the opportunity for individuals to experience redemption and change.

Practicing Showing Compassion:

Put Yourself in Their Shoes: Try to understand the perspective and struggles of those who have wronged you.

Respond with Kindness: Respond to their needs with kindness, whether through acts of service, support, or simply listening.

Pray for Them: Lift them up in prayer, asking God to work in their lives and bring about positive change.

Let Go of Judgment: Release judgment and offer forgiveness, extending grace and the possibility of transformation.

Set Healthy Boundaries: While showing compassion, maintain healthy boundaries to protect yourself.

The Power of Showing Compassion:

1. **Healing and Reconciliation:** Compassion can lead to healing and reconciliation in strained relationships.
2. **Transformation:** It has the potential to facilitate transformation in the lives of those who have wronged you.
3. **Witness to God's Love:** Compassion serves as a compelling witness to the transformative power of God's love.
4. **Overcoming Evil with Good:** Responding with compassion

counters hostility and revenge, exemplifying the teaching of overcoming evil with good.

5. **Reflecting Christ's Character:** It reflects the character of Christ, who demonstrated compassion and love even to His enemies.

6. **Personal Growth:** Practicing compassion contributes to your personal growth and spiritual maturity.

Showing compassion to those who have wronged you is a challenging but transformative aspect of discipleship. It mirrors the love and mercy of Christ, offering the hope of redemption and reconciliation. As you extend compassion, you become an agent of God's grace and a testament to the power of His love to change hearts and lives.

In this chapter, we have explored the concept of grace and how it shapes your journey as a disciple. Grace is not only the means by which you are saved but also the transformative power that enables you to live a life of repentance, forgiveness, and love. As you continue on the road to discipleship, may you experience the fullness of God's grace and allow it to guide your interactions with others, transforming you into a reflection of His love and mercy.

Chapter 5: Living a Life of Service

SERVICE IS AT THE HEART of discipleship. In this chapter, we will explore the profound call to serve others as a disciple of Jesus. You will discover how to use your unique gifts and talents to make a positive impact in your community and the world.

The Call to Service

Service is at the heart of discipleship. Jesus Himself set the example of humble service, and as His follower, you are called to follow in His footsteps.

The Significance of the Call to Service:

1. **Imitating Christ:** Serving others is a way to imitate the servant-hearted nature of Jesus.
2. **Fulfilling the Great Commandment:** It fulfills the commandment to love your neighbor as yourself.
3. **Demonstrating Love:** Service is a tangible way to demonstrate your love for God and others.
4. **Bringing God's Kingdom:** Through service, you participate in bringing God's kingdom values to the world.

Principles of the Call to Service:

Humility: Approach service with humility, recognizing that you are serving for the glory of God, not personal recognition.

Selflessness: Be selfless in your service, putting the needs of others before your own.

Compassion: Serve with a compassionate heart, empathizing with the struggles and needs of those you serve.

Consistency: Maintain a consistent attitude of service in both small and large acts.

Availability: Be available to serve as opportunities arise, not just when it's convenient.

Multiplying Impact: Encourage others to join you in service, multiplying the impact of your efforts.

The Power of the Call to Service:

1. **Transformation:** Serving others transforms both the server and the one being served, fostering personal growth and healing.
2. **Unity in the Church:** A community that serves together experiences unity and a sense of purpose.
3. **Witness to God's Love:** Service becomes a powerful witness to God's love and care for humanity.
4. **Addressing Needs:** It addresses the physical, emotional, and spiritual needs of individuals and communities.
5. **Advancing God's Kingdom:** Through service, you actively participate in advancing God's kingdom on earth.
6. **Joy and Fulfillment:** Serving others brings joy and fulfillment as you experience the joy of making a positive impact.

The call to service is not limited to specific roles or positions but extends to all aspects of life. It involves a heart attitude of humility, love, and compassion in your interactions with others. As you respond to this call, you embody the essence of discipleship and become a reflection of Christ's love in the world.

A Reflection of Jesus: Jesus set the ultimate example of service. In Mark 10:45, He says, "For even the Son of Man came not to be served but to serve, and to give his life as a ransom for many." As a disciple, you are called to emulate His selfless and sacrificial service.

The Significance of Reflecting Jesus in Service:

Imitating Christ: Reflecting Jesus in service means imitating His selflessness and humility.

Living Out His Teachings: It involves living out His teachings, which emphasize love, compassion, and servanthood.

Sacrificial Love: Reflecting Jesus in service demonstrates sacrificial love for others.

Bringing Glory to God: It brings glory to God as you embody the character of Christ in your actions.

PRINCIPLES OF REFLECTING Jesus in Service:

1. **Selflessness:** Serve with a selfless heart, putting the needs of others above your own.
2. **Humility:** Approach service with humility, recognizing your dependence on God's grace.
3. **Compassion:** Serve with a compassionate heart, seeking to alleviate the suffering of others.
4. **Sacrifice:** Be willing to make sacrifices for the well-being and benefit of those you serve.
5. **Obedience to His Example:** Obey Christ's example of service, even when it involves personal cost.

The Power of Reflecting Jesus in Service:

Transformation: Reflecting Jesus in service transforms your character and draws you closer to Christ.

Impact: Your service has a profound impact on the lives of those you serve.

Witness to God's Love: It serves as a powerful witness to the love and grace of God.

Unity in the Church: Reflecting Jesus in service fosters unity and a sense of purpose within the faith community.

Advancing God's Kingdom: Through service, you actively participate in advancing God's kingdom on earth.

Joy and Fulfillment: Reflecting Jesus in service brings joy and fulfillment as you experience the privilege of serving as He did.

Reflecting Jesus in service is not about performing grandiose acts of charity but embodying His love, humility, and selflessness in your daily interactions with others. As you do so, you become a living testimony to the transformative power of Christ's example and a channel of His love to a hurting world.

A Commandment: Jesus commanded His disciples to serve others. In John 13:14-15, He instructs, "If I then, your Lord and Teacher, have washed your feet, you also ought to wash one another's feet. For I have given you an example, that you also should do just as I have done to you."

The Significance of Serving as a Commandment:

1. **Obedience to Christ:** Serving others is an act of obedience to Christ's explicit command.
2. **Discipleship Mandate:** It is an essential aspect of

discipleship, following Jesus' example and teachings.

3. **Fulfilling His Expectations:** Serving as a commandment fulfills the expectations of a devoted follower of Christ.
4. **Demonstrating Love:** It demonstrates your love for God and your commitment to live out His Word.

Principles of Serving as a Commandment:

Submission: Obey the command to serve willingly and with a heart of submission to Christ.

Consistency: Make service a consistent and integral part of your discipleship journey.

Teaching Through Action: Use your service as a teaching tool to show others the way of Christ.

Servant Leadership: Embrace servant leadership, leading by example in your service to others.

THE POWER OF SERVING as a Commandment:

Obedience: Serving as a commandment demonstrates your obedience to Christ's teachings.

Discipleship Growth: It fosters growth and maturity in your discipleship journey.

Unity in the Church: Serving as a commandment promotes unity and a sense of shared purpose within the faith community.

Impact: Your obedient service has a meaningful and lasting impact on the lives of those you serve.

Witness to Christ's Lordship: It bears witness to Christ's lordship over your life and your commitment to follow His example.

Alignment with God's Will: Serving in obedience aligns your actions with God's will and His desire for you to serve others.

Serving as a commandment underscores the importance of not just occasional acts of service but a lifestyle characterized by humble service to others. It is a tangible expression of your commitment to follow Christ and a demonstration of your love for both God and your fellow human beings.

DISCOVERING YOUR GIFTS and Talents

Discovering and using your spiritual gifts and talents is a vital part of service within the body of Christ and the world. Each disciple has unique gifts and abilities given by God to contribute to the growth of the Church and the well-being of humanity.

The Significance of Discovering Your Gifts and Talents:

Fulfilling Your Role: Discovering your gifts enables you to fulfill your role within the body of Christ effectively.

Stewardship: It reflects responsible stewardship of the gifts God has entrusted to you.

Effective Service: Identifying your gifts enhances your effectiveness in serving others and advancing God's kingdom.

Unity and Diversity: Recognizing the diversity of gifts within the Church promotes unity and a holistic approach to ministry.

Principles of Discovering Your Gifts and Talents:

1. **Self-Examination:** Engage in self-examination and reflection to discern your unique gifts and talents.
2. **Seek Guidance:** Seek guidance and mentorship from mature believers and leaders within your faith community.
3. **Experiment and Serve:** Experiment with different forms of service to discover where your gifts align best.
4. **Feedback:** Be open to feedback from others regarding your strengths and areas of service.

The Power of Discovering Your Gifts and Talents:

Effective Service: Discovering your gifts enables you to serve more effectively and make a greater impact.

Joy and Fulfillment: Serving in areas that align with your gifts brings joy and fulfillment.

Unity in the Church: It promotes unity and cooperation within the body of Christ as each member contributes their unique gifts.

Ministry Diversity: Recognizing a variety of gifts leads to a diverse range of ministries that meet different needs.

Growth and Maturity: Discovering and using your gifts fosters personal growth and spiritual maturity.

God's Glory: Ultimately, discovering your gifts and using them brings glory to God as you use what He has given you for His purposes.

Your gifts and talents are not for personal gain but for the service of others and the advancement of God's kingdom. As you discover and utilize them, you play a crucial role in building up the Church and sharing God's love with the world.

Unique Abilities: Each disciple has unique gifts and talents. Part of your journey is discovering these gifts and how you can use them for the benefit of others. Romans 12:6-8 highlights the diversity of gifts within the body of believers.

The Power of Embracing Unique Abilities:

Effective Service: Embracing your unique abilities enables you to serve more effectively and make a greater impact.

Joy and Fulfillment: Serving in areas that align with your unique abilities brings joy and fulfillment.

Unity in the Church: It promotes unity and cooperation within the body of Christ as each member contributes their unique gifts.

Diverse Ministries: Recognizing a variety of unique abilities leads to a diverse range of ministries that meet different needs.

Personal Growth: Embracing your unique abilities fosters personal growth and spiritual maturity.

God's Glory: Ultimately, embracing your unique abilities and using them brings glory to God as you fulfill His purpose for your life.

Your unique abilities are not accidental but part of God's intentional plan for His Church. By embracing and using them, you contribute to the health and growth of the body of Christ, serving as a valuable member of the faith community.

THE SIGNIFICANCE OF Unique Abilities:

1. **God's Design:** Your unique abilities are part of God's intentional design for His body, the Church.

2. **Complementing Others:** Your gifts and talents complement those of others, creating a holistic and balanced ministry.
3. **Service and Edification:** Discovering your unique abilities enables you to serve others and contribute to their edification.
4. **Fulfilling Your Calling:** It helps you fulfill your calling and purpose within the body of Christ.

Principles of Embracing Unique Abilities:

Self-Discovery: Engage in self-discovery and self-reflection to identify your unique gifts and talents.

Self-Discovery: Engaging in Self-Discovery for Identifying Your Unique Gifts and Talents

Self-discovery is a crucial step in identifying your unique gifts and talents. It involves introspection, reflection, and a deeper understanding of who you are in Christ. Here are practical steps to help you in the process of self-discovery:

1. Reflect on Your Passions and Interests:

Take time to think about the activities, subjects, or causes that genuinely excite and interest you. Your passions often align with your gifts and talents.

2. Assess Your Strengths and Weaknesses:

Identify your strengths and weaknesses, both in your character and skills. Consider what comes naturally to you and where you may need improvement.

3. Seek Feedback from Others:

Ask close friends, family, mentors, or members of your faith community for their insights. Sometimes, others can see your gifts more clearly than you can.

4. Review Your Life Experiences:

Reflect on moments in your life where you felt particularly fulfilled, accomplished, or in your element. These instances can provide clues to your gifts and talents.

5. Take Spiritual Gift Assessments:

Many resources and assessments are available to help you identify your spiritual gifts. Utilizing spiritual gifts assessments is a practical step in identifying your spiritual gifts and talents. These assessments can offer valuable insights into how God has uniquely equipped you for service within your faith community and beyond. Here's how to effectively use them:

1. Locate Reliable Assessments:

Research and identify reputable spiritual gift assessments. Many churches and religious organizations offer these tools, and online resources are available as well.

2. Prepare for Assessment:

Before taking the assessment, set aside dedicated time for reflection and prayer. Approach it with an open heart and a desire to discover how God has gifted you.

3. Take the Assessment:

Complete the assessment honestly and thoughtfully. Answer questions based on your genuine experiences, preferences, and inclinations.

4. Interpret the Results:

After completing the assessment, carefully review the results. These typically identify your spiritual gift, sometimes ranking them by strength.

5. Seek Clarification:

If you have questions or are unsure about the results, seek clarification from a trusted mentor or leader within your faith community. They can help you understand and interpret the findings.

6. Reflect on the Implications:

Take time to reflect on how the identified spiritual gift align with your interests, passions, and current service roles.

7. Explore Opportunities:

Based on your spiritual gift, explore service opportunities within your faith community and consider how you can use your gifts to benefit others.

8. Discuss with Others:

Engage in conversations with fellow believers who have taken similar assessments. Share insights and learn from one another's experiences.

9. Revisit Periodically:

Revisit the spiritual gift assessment periodically, especially as you grow and mature in your discipleship journey. Your gifts may evolve or become more refined.

10. Pray for Guidance:

Pray for God's guidance and wisdom as you discern how to effectively use your spiritual gift for His purposes.

11. Align with Ministry Roles:

Seek ministry roles or areas of service that align with your identified spiritual gift. Your faith community leaders can help match you with suitable opportunities.

12. Embrace Diversity:

Remember that your spiritual gift is part of a diverse array of gifts within the body of Christ. Embrace the unique contributions of others and work collaboratively.

Using spiritual gift assessments can be a valuable tool in your discipleship journey. It not only helps you understand your unique gifting but also empowers you to serve more effectively and joyfully, contributing to the growth and health of your faith community and the broader community you serve. Assessments can provide valuable insights into how God has uniquely equipped you for service.

Remember that self-discovery is not a one-time event but a lifelong journey. As you uncover your unique gifts and talents, consider how you can use them to serve God and others, bringing fulfillment to your discipleship journey and contributing to the greater good within your faith community and the world.

Community Feedback: Seek feedback and guidance from your faith community to affirm and refine your understanding of your abilities.

The faith community can be a valuable source of feedback and guidance as you identify and refine your unique gifts and talents. Here's how to effectively seek feedback and support from your faith community:

1. Build Relationships:

Develop meaningful relationships within your faith community. Establishing trust and rapport with fellow believers creates a supportive environment for seeking feedback.

2. Share Your Journey:

Openly share your journey of self-discovery with trusted members of your faith community. Explain your desire to identify and use your gifts for God's glory.

3. Ask for Input:

Specifically ask for input regarding your strengths, talents, and areas where you might have made an impact. Encourage honest and constructive feedback.

4. Participate Actively:

Actively participate in your faith community's activities and ministries. This allows others to observe your skills and gifts in action.

5. Seek Mentorship:

Identify individuals within your faith community who are spiritually mature and experienced. Ask them to mentor you in discovering and refining your gift.

6. Attend Workshops and Classes:

Many faith communities offer workshops or classes on spiritual gifts and talents. Attend these to gain a better understanding and seek guidance.

7. Serve Alongside Others:

Engage in collaborative ministry efforts. Serving alongside others provides opportunities for mutual feedback and learning.

8. Embrace Accountability:

Be open to accountability. Allow fellow believers to gently challenge you and hold you accountable in your pursuit of using your gifts.

9. Use Spiritual Gift Assessments:

Your faith community may have resources, such as spiritual gifts assessments or tests, to help you identify your gifts more accurately. Take advantage of these tools.

10. Pray for Guidance:

Pray for guidance and discernment as you seek feedback. Ask God to lead you to the right individuals who can provide insights.

11. Be Open to Adjustments:

Be receptive to feedback, even if it challenges your initial perceptions of your gifts. Sometimes, others may see aspects of your abilities that you haven't recognized.

12. Express Gratitude:

Express gratitude to those who offer feedback and guidance. Show appreciation for their willingness to invest in your growth.

Remember that seeking feedback from your faith community is a collaborative effort. It not only helps you better understand your gifts but also fosters a sense of belonging and unity within your church or religious group. As you refine your understanding of your abilities, you'll be better equipped to serve both your faith community and the broader community, fulfilling your role as a disciple of Christ.

Experiment and Serve: Experiment with different forms of service to explore where your gifts align best.

Experimenting with different forms of service is a practical way to discover where your gifts and talents align best. Here are steps to guide your exploration:

1. Identify Service Opportunities:

Seek out a variety of service opportunities within your faith community and the wider community. Look for areas where your interests and passions align.

2. Volunteer for Diverse Roles:

Be open to volunteering for diverse roles, even those that might not initially seem like a perfect fit. Sometimes, you discover unexpected talents in the process.

3. Observe Your Impact:

Pay attention to how your service impacts others and the level of fulfillment it brings you. Reflect on which roles energize you and where you feel most effective.

4. Seek Feedback:

Ask for feedback from those you serve with and those you serve. Others can provide valuable insights into your strengths and areas for improvement.

5. Assess Your Joy and Satisfaction:

Consider which forms of service bring you joy and satisfaction. These feelings can be indicators of where your gifts align.

6. Evaluate Your Growth:

Assess how each form of service contributes to your personal growth and spiritual development. Some roles may challenge you in ways that lead to growth.

7. Pray for Discernment:

Pray for discernment and guidance as you experiment with different forms of service. Ask God to lead you to the areas where you can make the most significant impact.

8. Keep a Service Journal:

Maintain a journal to record your experiences, feelings, and observations while serving in various roles. This journal can help you track patterns and insights.

9. Seek Mentorship:

Consult mentors or experienced individuals in your faith community for advice on where your gifts may align best. Their wisdom can be invaluable.

10. Rotate Roles:

If possible, rotate through different roles over time. This can provide a well-rounded perspective on your gifts and talents.

11. Trust the Process:

Trust that the process of experimentation is a valuable part of your journey. It may take time to discover where your gifts align best.

12. Don't Fear Mistakes:

Don't be afraid to make mistakes or try something new. Mistakes are opportunities for learning and growth.

13. Evaluate and Refine:

Periodically evaluate and refine your service commitments based on what you've learned about your gifts and talents.

Remember that discovering where your gifts align best is a dynamic and evolving process. Your gifts may evolve over time, and new opportunities for service may arise as you grow in your discipleship journey. Embrace the journey of exploration, and trust that God will lead you to serve in ways that are most aligned with His purposes for your life.

SURRENDER TO GOD'S Leading: Be open to God's leading and guidance as you discover and use your unique abilities.

Surrendering to God's leading is a vital aspect of discovering and using your unique abilities and spiritual gifts effectively. Here's how to maintain an open heart and mind to God's guidance:

1. Prayer and Meditation:

Begin each day with prayer and meditation, asking God for guidance and discernment in identifying and using your unique abilities.

2. Seek God's Will:

Continually seek God's will in your life. Surrender your desires and plans to His higher purpose.

3. Read Scripture:

Study the Bible regularly to gain insight into God's character and His plan for your life. Scripture can provide clear guidance on how to use your gifts for His glory.

4. Listen in Silence:

Set aside quiet moments to listen to God's voice. He often speaks through a still, small voice or a prompting in your heart.

5. Be Open to Change:

Be flexible and open to change. God may lead you in unexpected directions or reveal new aspects of your abilities over time.

6. Seek Wise Counsel:

Consult with mentors, spiritual leaders, or trusted friends who can offer godly wisdom and guidance in your journey.

7. Follow Peace:

Pay attention to the peace that accompanies God's leading. If a decision or action brings a sense of peace and alignment with God's will, it may be a sign of His guidance.

8. Trust His Timing:

Trust that God's timing is perfect. Sometimes, He may delay the full revelation of your unique abilities until the right moment.

9. Be Patient:

Practice patience and perseverance. God's guidance may not always be immediate, and His plans may unfold gradually.

10. Embrace Detours:

Be open to detours and unexpected opportunities that may lead you to discover new aspects of your abilities and gifts.

11. Emulate Christ's Obedience:

Follow the example of Jesus in surrendering to God's will. His obedience, even in challenging circumstances, serves as a model for your own surrender.

12. Learn from Challenges:

Understand that challenges and setbacks can also be part of God's plan for your growth. Embrace them as opportunities for learning and refinement.

13. Remember God's Faithfulness:

Reflect on past experiences of God's faithfulness in your life. This can strengthen your trust in His guidance for your future.

14. Maintain a Grateful Heart:

Cultivate gratitude for the abilities and gifts God has entrusted to you. Gratitude can open your heart to His leadership.

Surrendering to God's leading is an ongoing process of trust and obedience. It requires humility and a willingness to relinquish control over your life's direction. By seeking His guidance and following His leadership, you'll find clarity and purpose in how to use your unique abilities and gifts for His glory and the benefit of others.

Passion and Compassion: Your passions and areas of deep compassion often align with your gifts. What moves your heart can guide you toward the areas of service where you can make the most significant impact.

Serving in Your Community

Serving in your community is an essential part of living out your faith and using your unique gifts and talents for the benefit of others. Here's how you can effectively serve in your community:

1. Identify Community Needs:

Take time to identify the specific needs within your local community. This could involve issues like homelessness, hunger, education, or healthcare.

2. Connect with Local Organizations:

Research and connect with local nonprofit organizations, charities, or community groups that are already addressing these needs. Find out how you can support their efforts.

3. Volunteer Your Time:

Offer your time and skills as a volunteer. Many community organizations rely on volunteers to carry out their mission.

4. Leverage Your Unique Abilities:

Consider how your unique abilities and gifts can be applied to address community needs. For example, if you have teaching skills, you might volunteer as a tutor.

5. Collaborate with Others:

Collaborate with like-minded individuals and organizations to maximize your impact. Working together often achieves greater results.

6. Build Relationships:

Get to know the people you are serving. Building relationships fosters a sense of community and allows you to better understand their needs.

7. Advocate for Change:

Advocate for systemic change where needed. Sometimes, addressing the root causes of community issues is just as important as providing immediate assistance.

8. Support Local Businesses:

Support local businesses and artisans whenever possible. This can stimulate the local economy and help small businesses thrive.

9. Be Consistent:

Make a commitment to consistent service. Regularly contributing your time and resources can have a lasting impact.

10. Pray for Your Community:

Pray for your community's well-being and transformation. Seek God's guidance in how you can be an instrument of His love and change.

11. Raise Awareness:

Raise awareness about community issues among your friends, family, and faith community. Encourage others to join you in making a difference.

12. Measure Impact:

Continually assess the impact of your service efforts. This allows you to adjust and ensure your contributions are meaningful.

13. Share Your Faith:

When appropriate, share your faith with those you serve. Your actions and words can be a powerful testimony to God's love.

---

14. BE HUMBLE:

Approach community service with humility, recognizing that you are serving others out of love and compassion, not for personal recognition.

15. Reflect on Your Calling:

Regularly reflect on your calling to serve in your community. Remind yourself of the purpose and motivation behind your actions.

16. Rest and Recharge:

Take time to rest and recharge. Burnout can be a real risk when engaging in community service, so ensure you maintain a healthy balance.

Serving in your community is a tangible way to live out your discipleship and be a light in the world. By using your unique gifts and talents to meet the needs of those around you, you fulfill Christ's command to love your neighbor and make a positive impact on the lives of others.

Local Outreach:

Your community is a place where you can directly impact the lives of those around you. You can serve in various ways, such as volunteering at local shelters, participating in neighborhood cleanups, or supporting community initiatives.

Building Relationships: Discipleship involves building meaningful relationships with those you serve. Get to know the people you serve on a personal level, showing them love and care.

Service Beyond Borders

Global Missions: While local service is essential, discipleship can also lead you to serve in other parts of the world. Engaging in global missions allows you to share the message of Christ's love and meet critical needs in different cultures.

Engaging in global missions is a powerful way to extend the reach of your discipleship journey and make a significant impact on a global scale. Here's how to effectively participate in global missions:

1. Pray for Guidance:

Begin by seeking God's guidance through prayer. Ask Him to reveal His calling for global missions in your life.

2. Identify Your Passion:

Reflect on your passions and interests. Consider what areas of global missions resonate with your heart, such as healthcare, education, poverty alleviation, or evangelism.

3. Research Mission Organizations:

Research reputable mission organizations that align with your mission interests and values. Ensure they have a track record of responsible and ethical work.

4. Connect with Experienced Missionaries:

Connect with experienced missionaries who can provide insights and guidance based on their experiences in the field.

5. PREPARE SPIRITUALLY:

Prepare yourself spiritually for the challenges of global missions. Strengthen your relationship with God through prayer, Bible study, and worship.

6. Seek Training and Education:

Depending on your role in global missions, seek relevant training and education to equip yourself for the work you'll be doing.

7. Fundraising and Financial Planning:

Develop a financial plan for your mission work. Consider fundraising, saving, or seeking support from your faith community.

8. Build a Support Team:

Form a support team of friends, family, and fellow believers who can pray for you, offer encouragement, and assist with logistics.

9. Cultural Sensitivity:

Learn about the culture and customs of the people you'll be serving. Cultural sensitivity is crucial for effective mission work.

10. Health and Safety:

Prioritize your health and safety. Ensure you have necessary vaccinations and medical preparations for the region you'll be serving in.

11. STAY CONNECTED:

Maintain communication with your support team and loved ones while in the field. Regular updates and connections provide emotional support.

12. Adaptability:

Be adaptable and open to the unexpected. Global missions often involve dealing with unforeseen challenges and circumstances.

13. Share the Gospel:

If your mission includes evangelism, be prepared to share the message of Christ's love with those you encounter. Build relationships and share your faith naturally.

14. Long-Term Commitment:

Consider the possibility of long-term commitment to global missions if it aligns with your calling and the needs of the community you serve.

15. Reflect and Learn:

Continually reflect on your experiences in global missions. Learn from both successes and challenges and use these insights to refine your approach.

16. Collaborate with Local Partners:

Collaborate with local churches and organizations in the regions you serve. Local partnerships can enhance the impact of your mission work.

ENGAGING IN GLOBAL missions is a transformative journey that allows you to share the message of Christ's love and meet critical needs in different cultures and communities. It requires dedication, preparation, and a heart that is open to serving and learning from others. By participating in global missions, you play a vital role in fulfilling the Great Commission and advancing God's kingdom worldwide.

Praying for and Supporting Global Causes: Even if you can't physically go on missions, you can support global causes through prayer and financial contributions. Your support can make a profound difference in the lives of those in need around the world.

The Joy of Serving

1. Joy and Contentment:

Serving others brings a genuine sense of joy and contentment. Witnessing the positive impact of your actions on someone's life can be deeply rewarding.

2. Purpose and Meaning:

Serving gives your life a sense of purpose and meaning. It helps you see beyond your own needs and desires and focus on the needs of others.

3. Spiritual Growth:

Engaging in acts of service fosters spiritual growth. It allows you to live out the teachings of Jesus and apply them to your daily life.

4. CONNECTION WITH God:

As you serve others, you draw closer to God. Your acts of service align with God's heart for compassion, love, and justice.

5. Building Relationships:

Serving often involves building meaningful relationships with those you serve and fellow volunteers. These connections can be a source of support and encouragement.

6. Gratitude and Humility:

Serving cultivates gratitude and humility. It reminds you of the blessings in your life and humbles you to see the needs of others.

7. Fulfillment of Your Calling:

For many disciples, serving is a fulfillment of their calling. It allows you to use your unique gifts and talents to make a positive impact in the world.

8. Leaving a Legacy:

Serving creates a lasting legacy. Your acts of kindness and service can have a ripple effect, influencing future generations.

9. Aligning with God's Will:

Serving others aligns with God's will for His followers. It reflects His character and His desire for us to love and care for one another.

---

10. COUNTERING SELFISHNESS:

Serving counters, the natural inclination toward selfishness. It challenges you to prioritize the needs of others and practice selflessness.

11. Fulfilling the Great Commission:

Through serving, you actively participate in fulfilling the Great Commission, spreading the message of Christ's love and salvation.

12. Bringing Light to the World:

Your acts of service shine as a light in a world that often feels dark and troubled. They demonstrate God's love and hope to others.

13. Encouragement and Inspiration:

Your service can encourage and inspire others to also engage in acts of kindness and service, creating a ripple effect of positive change.

14. Personal Transformation:

Serving can lead to personal transformation as you grow in compassion, empathy, and a deeper understanding of the needs of humanity.

In embracing a life of service, you not only enrich the lives of others but also experience the rich blessings of fulfillment, joy, and spiritual growth. Serving becomes an expression of your discipleship journey, a tangible way to live out your faith, and a source of deep connection with God and the world around you.

―――

FULFILLMENT: Serving others brings a deep sense of fulfillment. Jesus said in Acts 20:35, "It is more blessed to give than to receive." You'll find that serving brings joy, purpose, and a deeper connection with God.

Reflecting God's Love: Through your service, you become a tangible representation of God's love to the world. Your acts of kindness and compassion demonstrate the transformative power of Christ's love.

Strengthening Your Faith: Service is not only an expression of your faith but also a means of strengthening it. It deepens your understanding of God's heart for humanity and the transformative impact of His grace.

In this chapter, we have explored the call to live a life of service as a disciple of Jesus. By discovering your gifts and talents, serving in your community, and embracing global missions, you can fulfill the commandment to serve others and make a positive impact on the world. Service is not just an obligation but a privilege and a source of immense joy and spiritual growth on your discipleship journey.

Chapter 6: Facing Challenges and Trials

DISCIPLESHIP IS A JOURNEY filled with both joys and challenges. In this chapter, we will explore the reality that difficult times are a part of the discipleship journey. You'll learn practical strategies for navigating these challenges and growing stronger in your faith.

The Inevitability of Challenges

Challenges and trials are an inevitable part of the discipleship journey. While your faith and commitment to following Jesus are unwavering, you will undoubtedly face difficulties along the way. Here's how to navigate these challenges with resilience and faith:

1. Expect Trials:

Recognize that trials and challenges are a normal part of discipleship. Jesus Himself faced numerous challenges during His ministry.

2. Lean on God:

Turn to God for strength and guidance during difficult times. Pray fervently and seek His wisdom in navigating challenges.

3. Stay Grounded in Scripture:

Draw on the wisdom and encouragement found in the Bible. Many biblical figures faced trials and overcame them with faith.

4. Seek Support:

Don't hesitate to seek support and encouragement from your faith community and trusted friends. They can provide valuable guidance and a listening ear.

5. Embrace Perseverance:

Develop a mindset of perseverance. Understand that challenges can be opportunities for growth and refinement.

6. Trust God's Plan:

Trust that God has a purpose for the challenges you face. Even when you can't see the bigger picture, God is working for your good.

7. Maintain Hope:

Hold onto hope even during trials. Your hope in God's faithfulness will carry you through difficult times.

8. Practice Patience:

Practice patience in waiting for God's timing. Sometimes, challenges persist to test your faith and reliance on Him.

9. Surrender Control:

Surrender control to God and acknowledge that His ways are higher than your own. Trust that He is in control, even when circumstances seem uncertain.

10. Learn from Challenges:

View challenges as opportunities for learning and growth. Reflect on what you can gain from each trial.

11. Keep Your Eyes on Jesus:

Fix your eyes on Jesus, the ultimate example of faith and endurance. His life and teachings provide guidance for navigating challenges.

---

12. ENCOURAGE OTHERS:

As you overcome challenges, offer encouragement and support to fellow disciples who may be facing similar difficulties.

13. Maintain Perspective:

Keep a healthy perspective on challenges. While they may be challenging, they are temporary considering eternity.

14. Focus on Eternal Values:

Remember that discipleship is about pursuing eternal values. Challenges in this world are temporary, but your commitment to Christ is eternal.

15. Find Purpose in Challenges:

Seek to find purpose in your challenges. They can refine your character, deepen your faith, and prepare you for greater service.

16. Keep the Faith:

Above all, keep the faith. Your unwavering commitment to Christ will carry you through every challenge you encounter on your discipleship journey.

Embracing the inevitability of challenges is an integral part of discipleship. It's through these trials that your faith is tested and refined, ultimately strengthening your relationship with God and preparing you for the journey ahead. Remember that God is with you in every challenge, and His grace is sufficient to see you through.

Narrow Path: Jesus acknowledged that the path of discipleship is narrow and not without its difficulties (Matthew 7:13-14). Challenges are a natural part of your journey of faith.

A Narrow Path: Embracing the Challenges of Discipleship

As Jesus taught, the path of discipleship is indeed narrow and not without its challenges. In Matthew 7:13-14, He said, "Enter through the narrow gate. For wide is the gate and broad is the road that leads to destruction, and many enter through it. But small is the gate and narrow the road that leads to life, and only a few find it."

Here's how you can navigate the challenges of this narrow path:

1. Embrace the Narrowness:

Understand that the narrow path is the path of discipleship. It may not always be easy or popular, but it leads to life and a deeper relationship with God.

2. Count the Cost:

Consider the cost of discipleship as Jesus advised (Luke 14:28). Discipleship may require sacrifices, but the reward is eternal life.

3. Lean on God's Strength:

Rely on God's strength to walk the narrow path. You don't have to face challenges alone; God is with you.

4. SEEK WISDOM:

Seek wisdom and discernment in making decisions on this path. Proverbs 3:6 says, "In all your ways acknowledge him, and he will make your paths straight."

5. Find Support:

Surround yourself with a faith community that can provide support, encouragement, and accountability as you navigate the challenges of discipleship.

6. Focus on the Destination:

Keep your focus on the destination—eternal life with God. The challenges of the narrow path are temporary compared to the eternal reward.

7. Be Prepared for Opposition:

Be prepared for opposition and challenges from those who may not understand or share your faith. Respond with love and patience.

8. Persevere with Hope:

Persevere with hope, knowing that the difficulties you face on the narrow path are building character and deepening your faith.

9. Trust God's Guidance:

Trust in God's guidance and direction for your life. He knows the way and will lead you in paths of righteousness (Psalm 23:3).

---

10. SEEK CHRISTLIKENESS:

Ultimately, discipleship is about becoming more like Christ. Embrace the challenges as opportunities for spiritual growth and transformation.

11. Rest in God's Peace:

Find peace in the knowledge that you are walking in obedience to God's call. His peace can sustain you through every trial.

12. Share Your Journey:

Share your journey with others, both the joys and the challenges. Your testimony can inspire and encourage fellow disciples.

13. Remember the Reward:

Remember that the reward of eternal life with God is worth every challenge and difficulty you may encounter on the narrow path.

14. Keep the Faith:

Above all, keep the faith. Your unwavering commitment to following Jesus on the narrow path is a testament to your love for Him and your desire to live in accordance with His teachings.

Embracing the narrow path of discipleship, despite its challenges, is a courageous and rewarding journey. It leads to a deeper relationship with God, spiritual growth, and the promise of eternal life. As you walk this path, you are not alone; God is your constant companion, guiding you every step of the way.

Spiritual Warfare: The Apostle Paul reminds us that our struggle is not against flesh and blood but against spiritual forces (Ephesians 6:12). As a disciple, you may face spiritual battles and opposition.

As the Apostle Paul reminds us in Ephesians 6:12, our struggle is not merely against flesh and blood, but against spiritual forces. As a disciple of Jesus, you may indeed face spiritual battles and opposition. Here's how to navigate these challenges with faith and resilience:

1. Put on the Armor of God:

Follow Paul's advice in Ephesians 6:13-18 by putting on the whole armor of God. This spiritual armor includes truth, righteousness, the gospel of peace, faith, salvation, and the Word of God. It is your protection against spiritual attacks.

2. Pray Continually:

Maintain a lifestyle of prayer. Regular and fervent prayer keeps you connected to God and empowers you to face spiritual warfare.

3. Stand Firm in Your Faith:

Stand firm in your faith, knowing that God is greater than any spiritual force. Trust in His protection and guidance.

4. Resist the Devil:

As James 4:7 advises, "Submit yourselves, then, to God. Resist the devil, and he will flee from you." When faced with spiritual opposition, resist by drawing closer to God.

---

5. SEEK DELIVERANCE and Healing:

If you or someone you know is under spiritual attack, seek deliverance and healing through prayer, seeking the counsel of experienced spiritual leaders, and relying on God's power.

6. Stay Grounded in Scripture:

The Word of God is a powerful weapon against spiritual warfare. Keep yourself grounded in Scripture to discern truth and combat deception.

7. Maintain Accountability:

Stay accountable to your faith community and spiritual mentors. They can provide guidance and support during times of spiritual battle.

8. Guard Your Mind:

Guard your mind against negative and destructive thoughts. Fill your mind with thoughts that are pure, lovely, and praiseworthy (Philippians 4:8).

9. Avoid Occult Practices:

Steer clear of occult practices and anything that opens doors to spiritual darkness. Instead, focus on practices that draw you closer to God.

10. Lean on the Holy Spirit:

Rely on the power of the Holy Spirit dwelling within you. The Holy Spirit provides wisdom, discernment, and strength in times of spiritual warfare.

---

11. ENGAGE IN WORSHIP:

Worship and praise are potent weapons against spiritual opposition. Singing praises to God can drive away darkness and invite His presence.

12. Seek Spiritual Guidance:

If you encounter challenges beyond your understanding, seek guidance from experienced spiritual leaders who can provide insight and discernment.

13. Pray for Protection:

Regularly pray for God's protection over yourself, your loved ones, and your faith community. Ask for His angels to guard and watch over you.

14. Know Your Authority in Christ:

Understand your authority as a disciple of Christ. You have the authority to rebuke spiritual forces in Jesus' name.

15. Trust in God's Sovereignty:

Trust that God is ultimately in control. Even during spiritual battles, His plan and purpose will prevail.

Facing spiritual warfare as a disciple can be challenging but remember that your faith in Christ and your reliance on God's strength equip you to overcome. Through prayer, spiritual armor, and unwavering trust in God, you can stand firm against any spiritual opposition that may arise on your discipleship journey.

STRATEGIES FOR NAVIGATING Challenges on Your Discipleship Journey

Navigating challenges as a disciple is an essential part of your spiritual growth and journey of faith. Here are some strategies to help you navigate these challenges effectively:

1. Stay Connected to God:

Maintain a strong and consistent connection with God through prayer, meditation, and worship. Seek His guidance and wisdom in every challenge you face.

2. Lean on Scripture:

The Bible is your source of wisdom, comfort, and guidance. Regularly read and meditate on Scripture to find encouragement and solutions to your challenges.

3. Seek Counsel:

Don't hesitate to seek counsel from trusted mentors, pastors, or fellow believers. They can offer valuable perspectives and support.

4. Embrace Resilience:

Develop a resilient mindset that views challenges as opportunities for growth and learning. Embrace challenges as a means of becoming more like Christ.

5. Trust God's Timing:

Recognize that God's timing may not align with your own. Trust that His plans are perfect and that He is working all things together for your good.

---

6. CULTIVATE GRATITUDE:

Cultivate an attitude of gratitude. Even in challenging times, find reasons to be thankful and focus on the blessings in your life.

7. Maintain Perspective:

Keep a healthy perspective on challenges. Remember that they are temporary considering eternity. Your goal is to follow Christ faithfully.

8. Seek Support from Your Faith Community:

Your faith community can provide essential support during challenges. Share your struggles, seek prayer, and lean on one another for encouragement.

9. Practice Patience:

Practice patience in waiting for God's answers and solutions. Some challenges may take time to resolve.

10. Reflect and Learn:

Take time to reflect on the challenges you've overcome and the lessons you've learned. Use these experiences to grow in wisdom and faith.

11. Be Flexible:

Be open to God's leading and be flexible in your approach to challenges. Sometimes, His solutions may differ from your expectations.

------

12. FIND PURPOSE IN Challenges:

Seek to find purpose in your challenges. Consider how they can be used to serve others, bring glory to God, or deepen your relationship with Him.

13. Encourage Others:

As you overcome challenges, share your experiences with others. Your testimony can inspire and encourage fellow believers facing similar trials.

14. Rely on God's Strength:

Recognize your own limitations and rely on God's strength. He promises to be your refuge and strength in times of trouble (Psalm 46:1).

15. Be Persistent in Prayer:

Persist in prayer, especially during challenging times. Prayer connects you to God's power and invites His intervention.

16. Stay Humble:

Stay humble and recognize your dependence on God. Humility allows you to seek His guidance and surrender control.

17. Keep Your Eyes on Jesus:

Fix your eyes on Jesus, the author and perfecter of your faith (Hebrews 12:2). He is your ultimate source of strength and guidance.

CHALLENGES ARE A NATURAL part of the discipleship journey, but with faith, perseverance, and reliance on God, you can navigate them with grace and emerge stronger in your faith. Remember that God is with you every step of the way, providing the wisdom and strength you need to overcome every challenge that comes your way.

Prayer and Seeking God: In times of difficulty, turn to prayer and seek God's guidance and strength. Philippians 4:6-7 encourages you to "not be anxious about anything, but in everything by prayer and supplication with thanksgiving let your requests be made known to God."

Perseverance: The book of James speaks of the blessing that comes through endurance during trials (James 1:12). Keep moving forward, even when faced with adversity, trusting that God is working in and through your challenges.

Community Support: Lean on your faith community for support and encouragement. Galatians 6:2 reminds you to "bear one another's burdens, and so fulfill the law of Christ." Together, you can overcome challenges.

God's Promises: Meditate on God's promises in Scripture. They serve as anchors for your faith in turbulent times. One such promise is found in Romans 8:28: "And we know that in all things God works for the good of those who love him."

Finding Meaning in Challenges

Challenges, though often daunting, can hold profound meaning and purpose in your discipleship journey. Here's how to find meaning in these trials:

1. Growth and Maturity:

Challenges serve as opportunities for personal growth and spiritual maturity. They refine your character and deepen your faith, helping you become more like Christ.

2. Strengthened Faith:

When you overcome challenges with faith, your trust in God grows stronger. Your experiences become a testament to His faithfulness.

3. Empathy and Compassion:

Challenges can equip you with empathy and compassion for others facing similar difficulties. Your own struggles make you better equipped to offer support and understanding.

4. Greater Dependency on God:

Challenges remind you of your dependency on God. They draw you closer to Him as you seek His guidance and strength.

5. Surrender and Trust:

Challenges often require surrendering control and trusting in God's plan. This trust deepens your relationship with Him.

6. Purposeful Service:

Some challenges equip you for purposeful service. They prepare you to help others facing similar difficulties and to share the hope you've found in Christ.

7. Spiritual Refinement:

Challenges act as a refining fire, purifying your faith and burning away impurities. You emerge from these trials stronger and more steadfast.

8. A Deeper Understanding of God:

Challenges can lead to a deeper understanding of God's character. They reveal His faithfulness, grace, and love even in the midst of adversity.

9. Opportunity for Testimony:

Overcoming challenges provides you with a powerful testimony of God's work in your life. Sharing this testimony can inspire and encourage others.

10. Aligning with God's Will:

Facing challenges can help align your life more closely with God's will. You may discover new callings or directions for your discipleship journey.

11. Countercultural Witness:

Your response to challenges can serve as a countercultural witness to the world. It demonstrates the peace and hope that come from faith in Christ.

---

12. ETERNAL PERSPECTIVE:

Challenges remind you of the eternal perspective. They encourage you to focus on the things that matter most considering eternity.

13. A Closer Walk with God:

Challenges can lead to a closer walk with God. Amid difficulties, you may experience His presence and comfort in profound ways.

14. Embracing God's Purposes:

Trust that God has a purpose for every challenge you face, even if you can't see it immediately. He is working all things together for your good (Romans 8:28).

15. Perseverance and Endurance:

Challenges build perseverance and endurance, qualities that are essential for discipleship. You learn to press on even when the path is tough.

16. A Life of Witness:

Ultimately, your entire life, including its challenges, becomes a witness to the transformative power of Christ. Your discipleship journey inspires others to seek Him.

Embracing the meaning and purpose behind challenges transforms them from obstacles into opportunities for spiritual growth, service, and a deeper relationship with God. Trust that God is with you in every trial, guiding you toward a life that reflects His love and grace.

SPIRITUAL GROWTH: Challenges can be opportunities for spiritual growth. James 1:2-4 teaches that trials produce endurance, character, and maturity in your faith.

James 1:2-4 offers profound insight into how challenges can be transformative in your discipleship journey: "Consider it pure joy, my brothers and sisters, whenever you face trials of many kinds, because you know that the testing of your faith produces perseverance. Let perseverance finish its work so that you may be mature and complete, not lacking anything."

Here's how to view challenges as opportunities for spiritual growth:

1. Embrace Joy in Trials:

Begin by changing your perspective. Embrace the idea that challenges, though difficult, can lead to spiritual growth and a deeper walk with God.

2. Develop Perseverance:

Challenges require perseverance. As you endure, your faith becomes more resilient, and you learn to trust God even in the midst of difficulties.

3. Character Building:

Challenges refine your character. They reveal areas that need growth and transformation, and they provide opportunities for you to become more Christlike.

4. Patience and Endurance:

Challenges teach patience and endurance. These qualities are essential for your discipleship journey, helping you remain steadfast in your faith.

5. Trust in God's Purpose:

Trust that God has a purpose in allowing challenges. He is using them to shape you into the person He intends you to be.

6. Seek Wisdom:

When facing challenges, ask God for wisdom (James 1:5). Seek His guidance on how to navigate the difficulties and grow through them.

7. Reflect and Learn:

Take time to reflect on the lessons learned from challenges. What have you discovered about yourself and your relationship with God?

8. Persevere with Hope:

Persevere with hope, knowing that the challenges you face are not in vain. They are part of God's plan for your spiritual growth.

9. Lean on God's Strength:

Rely on God's strength to help you overcome challenges. His grace is sufficient for you (2 Corinthians 12:9).

10. Encourage Others:

Share your experiences of spiritual growth through challenges with others. Your testimony can inspire and encourage fellow believers on their journeys.

11. Keep Your Eyes on Jesus:

Keep your focus on Jesus, the ultimate example of spiritual growth and perseverance (Hebrews 12:2).

12. Foster a Teachable Spirit:

Be open to learning and growing through challenges. A teachable spirit is key to spiritual growth.

13. Be Patient with Yourself:

Understand that spiritual growth is a lifelong process. Be patient with yourself as you navigate challenges and seek transformation.

Challenges, though challenging, are indeed opportunities for spiritual growth and maturity. Through faith, perseverance, and reliance on God, you can emerge from trials stronger, wiser, and more deeply connected to your Creator.

Testing and Refinement: Just as gold is refined in the fire, your faith can be refined through challenges (1 Peter 1:7). God uses difficulties to purify and strengthen your faith.

A Witness to Others: Your response to challenges can be a powerful testimony to those around you. In difficult times, your faith can shine as a beacon of hope and resilience.

Trusting in God's Sovereignty: Finding Peace in His Control

Trusting in God's sovereignty is a foundational aspect of navigating challenges as a disciple. Here's how to embrace this trust:

1. Acknowledge God's Sovereignty:

Start by acknowledging that God is sovereign over all things. Nothing happens without His knowledge or permission.

2. Surrender Control:

Surrender your need for control. Recognize that God's plan is far greater than your own, and trust His wisdom.

3. Pray for Trust:

Pray for the strength to trust in God's sovereignty, even when you don't understand His ways.

4. Reflect on His Track Record:

Reflect on past experiences where God's sovereignty brought about good, even in challenging circumstances.

5. Seek Wisdom:

Ask for wisdom to discern God's sovereign will in your challenges. Seek His guidance on how to respond.

6. Remember Romans 8:28:

Meditate on Romans 8:28: "And we know that in all things God works for the good of those who love him, who have been called according to his purpose."

7. Trust His Timing:

Understand that God's timing may differ from yours. Trust that He knows the best time for every circumstance.

8. Rest in His Love:

Rest in the assurance of God's love. His sovereignty is rooted in His perfect love for you.

9. Let Go of Anxiety:

Release anxiety about the future. Trust that God holds your future in His hands.

10. Lean on His Strength:

In moments of weakness, lean on God's strength. He promises to be your refuge and strength (Psalm 46:1).

11. Find Peace in Surrender:

Find peace in surrendering your challenges to God. Let go of the burden and allow Him to carry it for you.

12. Share Your Struggles:

Share your struggles with others, both for support and to testify to God's faithfulness in challenging times.

13. Focus on Eternity:

Keep an eternal perspective. Remember that God's ultimate plan is for your eternal well-being.

14. Trust in His Promises:

Trust in God's promises. He has promised to be with you always, even in the midst of challenges (Matthew 28:20).

15. Be Patient:

Be patient as you wait on God's plan to unfold. His timing is perfect.

16. Cultivate Contentment:

Cultivate contentment with the knowledge that God is in control. You can find joy and peace in this trust.

17. Rejoice in His Sovereignty:

Rejoice in the sovereignty of God. It is a source of security and comfort in an uncertain world.

Trusting in God's sovereignty allows you to find peace and security in the midst of life's challenges. It's a cornerstone of your discipleship journey, reminding you that you serve a God who is always in control, always loving, and always working for your good.

God's Control: Remember that God is sovereign and in control, even in the midst of challenges. Proverbs 19:21 reminds you that "Many are the plans in a person's heart, but it is the LORD's purpose that prevails."

Embracing God's Will: Surrendering to God's will, even when it leads through challenging circumstances, is an act of faith. Jesus demonstrated this when He prayed in the Garden of Gethsemane (Matthew 26:39).

Hope in Christ: Your hope and strength come from Christ. In John 16:33, Jesus assures you, "In this world, you will have trouble. But take heart! I have overcome the world."

In this chapter, we have explored the inevitability of challenges in discipleship and provided practical strategies for navigating them. Challenges can be opportunities for growth, testing, and a deeper understanding of God's sovereignty. By relying on prayer, perseverance, community, and God's promises, you can face difficulties with resilience and faith, ultimately growing stronger in your discipleship journey.

Chapter 7: Community and Fellowship

DISCIPLESHIP IS NOT a solitary endeavor; it thrives in the context of community and fellowship. In this chapter, we will delve into the significance of community and fellowship in your journey as a disciple of Jesus.

In this chapter, you will discover the profound impact of community on your discipleship journey and how it can empower you to grow in faith, serve others, and find joy in fellowship.

The Power of Community

Community and fellowship are essential aspects of your discipleship journey. Here, we'll explore the significance of community in your walk with Christ and how it can provide you with the support, encouragement, and spiritual growth you need.

No one can walk the road to discipleship alone. In this chapter, we'll explore the importance of community and fellowship, helping you find the support and encouragement you need in your journey.

1. Created for Community:

Understand that God designed humans for community. In Genesis 2:18, God said, "It is not good for the man to be alone." You are meant to live in fellowship with others.

2. Strength in Numbers:

Recognize the strength in numbers. Ecclesiastes 4:9-12 emphasizes the value of companionship and support, stating that two are better than one because they can help each other in times of need.

3. Iron Sharpens Iron:

Proverbs 27:17 tells us, "As iron sharpens iron, so one person sharpens another." In a community of believers, you can challenge, encourage, and sharpen one another in your faith.

4. Mutual Encouragement:

Hebrews 10:24-25 encourages believers to "spur one another on toward love and good deeds" and not to give up meeting together. Regular gatherings provide opportunities for mutual encouragement.

5. Shared Burdens:

Galatians 6:2 reminds us to "carry each other's burdens," fulfilling the law of Christ. In a community, you can find support during challenging times.

6. Accountability:

Accountability is vital in discipleship. Proverbs 27:6 says, "Wounds from a friend can be trusted." Accountability helps you stay on course and grow in your faith.

7. Learning and Growth:

In a faith community, you could learn from others, share experiences, and grow together in your understanding of God's Word.

8. Service and Outreach:

Being part of a faith community enables you to engage in meaningful service and outreach efforts, putting your faith into action.

9. Worship and Fellowship:

Gathering with fellow believers for worship and fellowship is a source of spiritual nourishment and joy. It reminds you that you are part of a larger family in Christ.

10. Support in Trials:

Ecclesiastes 4:10 acknowledges that when one falls, the other can help. In times of trials, your community can provide the support and encouragement you need.

11. Sharing Your Gifts:

Your unique gifts and talents are meant to benefit the body of believers. In community, you can use your gifts to serve and bless others.

12. Prayer and Intercession:

Praying together strengthens the bond of community and allows you to lift one another up in prayer. It's a powerful way to support each other.

13. Diversity and Unity:

Embrace the diversity within your faith community. Different backgrounds and perspectives can enrich your understanding of God's truth.

14. Forgiveness and Reconciliation:

In a community of believers, you learn the importance of forgiveness and reconciliation, following Christ's example.

15. Joy in Fellowship:

Acts 2:46 describes the early believers as "continuing daily with one accord in the temple, and breaking bread from house to house, they ate their food with gladness and simplicity of heart." Fellowship with other believers brings joy and simplicity to your life.

16. A Witness to the World:

Your loving and supportive community can be a powerful witness to the world, showing the transformative power of Christ's love.

Created for Community:

From the beginning, God designed us for community. In Genesis 2:18, He declared, "It is not good for the man to be alone." We are meant to share our faith journey with others.

The Body of Christ: The Apostle Paul describes believers as the "body of Christ" in 1 Corinthians 12:27. Just as each part of a body has a unique role, every member of the Christian community plays a vital role in supporting and encouraging one another.

Benefits of Community and Fellowship

Support and Encouragement: In moments of doubt, discouragement, or difficulty, your faith community provides a network of support and encouragement. Hebrews 10:24-25 encourages you to "consider how we may spur one another on toward love and good deeds, not giving up meeting together."

The Body of Christ: A Metaphor for Community

The metaphor of the "body of Christ" found in 1 Corinthians 12:27 beautifully illustrates the interdependence and unity within the Christian community:

Interdependence: Just as different parts of the human body have distinct functions and rely on each other to function properly, members of the Christian community have unique gifts and roles that contribute to the health and growth of the whole. Your individual strengths and abilities are meant to complement and support those of others.

Unity: The body of Christ metaphor emphasizes the unity among believers. In Christ, you are part of a unified and interconnected body, bound together by a common faith and purpose. This unity transcends differences and divisions, fostering a sense of belonging and mutual care.

Equality: Regardless of your role or function within the body, every member is equally valuable and necessary. Just as the smallest body parts are indispensable, every believer, regardless of their perceived significance, is vital to the overall health and effectiveness of the Christian community.

Mutual Support: The body of Christ concept highlights the importance of mutual support and care. Just as one part of the body responds to the needs of another in times of injury or illness, Christians are called to support and care for one another in times of difficulty and need.

Diversity: The body metaphor celebrates diversity within the Christian community. Just as the body consists of various organs and tissues, each with its own unique function, the Christian community is made up of individuals with diverse backgrounds, talents, and experiences. This diversity enriches the community and enhances its ability to fulfill its mission.

Common Purpose: The body of Christ has a shared purpose – to honor God, serve others, and proclaim the message of Christ's love and salvation. Each member's unique contribution aligns with this overarching purpose, working together to fulfill the Great Commission and advance God's kingdom.

Leadership and Servanthood: Leaders within the Christian community are called to serve as servant-leaders, modeling the humility and selflessness demonstrated by Christ. They provide guidance and direction while serving the needs of the body.

Understanding the body of Christ metaphor reminds you that your Christian journey is not solitary but communal. Your participation in a faith community is an essential aspect of your discipleship, allowing you to thrive in your faith, support others, and collectively fulfill the mission of the Church.

Learning and Growth: Being part of a faith community provides opportunities for learning and spiritual growth. Through teaching, discussion, and shared experiences, you can deepen your understanding of God's Word.

Accountability: Accountability is essential for growth in discipleship. James 5:16 encourages you to "confess your sins to one another and pray for one another, that you may be healed." Accountability helps you stay on track and live a life aligned with your faith.

Worship and Celebration: Gathering with fellow believers for worship and celebration is a source of spiritual nourishment and joy. It reminds you of the larger family you are a part of and the goodness of God.

Gathering with fellow believers for worship and celebration is a central and uplifting aspect of your life in a faith community. Here's how it nourishes your spirit and brings joy:

Communal Worship: Worshiping together amplifies the sense of God's presence. As you join your voices in praise, it creates a powerful collective worship experience that draws you closer to God.

Remembrance and Gratitude: Worship services often include elements like communion or the Lord's Supper. These acts of remembrance and gratitude help you reflect on Christ's sacrifice and the depth of God's love.

Recharge and Renewal: Worship is a time for spiritual recharging. It rejuvenates your faith and strengthens your connection with God. It's like a spiritual "recharge" that equips you to face the challenges of life.

Proclamation of Truth: Worship services include the proclamation of God's Word, reinforcing your understanding of biblical truths and providing spiritual guidance.

Fellowship and Unity: Worship gatherings foster fellowship and unity among believers. Sharing in the worship experience deepens your sense of belonging to the body of Christ.

Corporate Prayer: Public prayers during worship include intercession for various needs. It reminds you of the importance of praying for one another and the broader community.

Joyful Celebration: Celebrating God's goodness and faithfulness through music, song, and praise lifts your spirits and reminds you of the reasons for rejoicing.

Hearing God's Word: The preaching of God's Word during worship provides insights, encouragement, and spiritual growth. It equips you to live out your faith in practical ways.

A Weekly Rhythm: Regular worship attendance establishes a weekly rhythm of spiritual nourishment. It offers a consistent opportunity to reset your focus on God.

Support and Encouragement: When facing challenges, being part of a worshiping community ensures you have a support system. You can draw strength and encouragement from fellow believers.

Corporate Testimonies: Hearing testimonies and stories of God's work in the lives of others bolsters your faith and reminds you of the power of God to transform.

Alignment with God's Heart: Worship aligns your heart with God's heart. It redirects your focus from earthly concerns to eternal priorities.

Reflecting God's Character: Through worship, you reflect God's character of love, holiness, and praise. It's a response to His greatness and a declaration of His worthiness.

A Taste of Heaven: Worship gives you a taste of the eternal worship that will occur in heaven. It's a foretaste of the joy and unity you'll experience in God's presence for eternity.

Gratitude and Contentment: Worship services often include moments of thanksgiving, fostering gratitude and contentment in your heart.

Renewed Purpose: Worship can renew your sense of purpose in following Christ and serving others. It reminds you of the calling to be a light in the world.

In summary, participating in worship and celebration within a faith community provides spiritual nourishment, reinforces biblical truths, and fosters joy and unity. It is a vital part of your discipleship journey, helping you grow in your faith and deepen your relationship with God and fellow believers,

Finding a Faith Community

Finding a faith community that aligns with your beliefs, values, and spiritual needs is a crucial step in your discipleship journey. Seek a community where you can grow in faith, find support and encouragement, and serve alongside like-minded believers. Look for a place where you can worship, learn, and fellowship together, nurturing your relationship with God and fostering spiritual growth. Whether it's a local church, a small group, or an online community, the right faith community can be a source of strength and inspiration on your road to discipleship.

Local Church: One of the most common ways to find a faith community is by attending a local church. Look for a church that aligns with your beliefs and values, and actively engage in its activities and gatherings.

Small Groups: Many churches offer small groups or Bible studies where you can build deeper relationships and engage in meaningful discussions.

Online Communities: In today's digital age, you can also find faith communities online. These can be a valuable supplement to your in-person interactions.

Being a Positive Member of Your Faith Community

Being a positive member of your faith community is not only about receiving support and encouragement but also about contributing to the spiritual well-being of others. Here are two key aspects to consider:

1. Active Participation: Engage actively in the life of your faith community. Attend worship services, join small groups, and participate in events and activities. Your presence and involvement strengthen the sense of community and provide opportunities for others to get to know you and vice versa. Actively participating in the various aspects of community life allows you to build deeper relationships, share your gifts and talents, and make a meaningful impact in the lives of fellow believers.

2. Servant Leadership: Embrace the spirit of servant leadership. Look for opportunities to serve and support others within your faith community. Whether it's volunteering for a ministry, offering a listening ear to someone in need, or simply extending acts of kindness, your willingness to serve reflects the love of Christ. By embodying servant leadership, you inspire and encourage others to do the same, fostering a culture of mutual care and support within your faith community. Your positive contributions can make a significant difference in creating a vibrant and thriving spiritual environments for all.

<hr>

INCORPORATING ACTIVE participation and a servant leadership mindset into your role within the faith community not only benefits those around you but also deepens your own discipleship journey. It aligns with Christ's call to love and serve one another, demonstrating the transformative power of faith in action within your community.

Active Participation: Be an active member of your faith community by attending meetings, volunteering, and participating in activities.

Encouragement: Encourage others in their faith journeys. Hebrews 3:13 advises you to "encourage one another daily."

Conflict Resolution: Conflicts can arise in any community. Approach conflicts with grace, humility, and a desire for reconciliation, as outlined in Matthew 18:15-17.

Servant Leadership: Be willing to serve and lead when called. Jesus modeled servant leadership, and you can follow His example in your community.

In this chapter, we have explored the importance of community and fellowship in your journey as a disciple. Being part of a faith community provides you with support, encouragement, accountability, and opportunities for growth. Finding and actively participating in a faith community is an integral aspect of discipleship, enabling you to thrive in your faith journey as you walk alongside others who share your commitment to following Jesus.

Chapter 8: Sharing Your Faith

AS A DISCIPLE, ONE of your primary responsibilities is to share the good news of Jesus Christ with others. In this chapter, we will discuss effective ways to share your faith and be a light in your sphere of influence.

The Great Commission

The Great Commission, found in Matthew 28:19-20, is a foundational directive for every disciple of Jesus:

"Go therefore and make disciples of all nations, baptizing them in the name of the Father and of the Son and of the Holy Spirit, teaching them to observe all that I have commanded you. And behold, I am with you always, to the end of the age." (Matthew 28:19-20 ESV)

These words from Jesus emphasize the mission of discipleship – to go, make disciples, baptize, and teach others to follow His teachings. They remind you that as a disciple, you have a crucial role in spreading the message of God's love, grace, and salvation to all people, drawing them into a relationship with Christ. Embracing the Great Commission is an integral part of your discipleship journey, fulfilling the call to be a light in the world and make an eternal impact.

A Command from Jesus: Before His ascension, Jesus gave His disciples the Great Commission in Matthew 28:18-20. He instructed them to "go and make disciples of all nations." This command applies to all disciples, including you.

SHARING THE GOSPEL: Sharing your faith involves proclaiming the gospel message—the good news of salvation through Jesus Christ. This message is centered on Jesus' life, death, and resurrection.

Effective Ways to Share Your Faith

Sharing your faith is an essential part of being a disciple. Here are some effective ways to do so:

1. Personal Testimony: Share your personal testimony of how you came to faith in Christ. Your story is a powerful tool to illustrate the transformative power of the gospel.

2. Build Relationships: Develop genuine relationships with non-believers. Show them love, care, and compassion, and be ready to share your faith when the opportunity arises.

3. Listen Actively: Listen to others and understand their questions and concerns. Address their doubts with empathy and respect.

4. Use Scripture: Use relevant Bible verses to support your conversations. For example, John 3:16 is a great verse to explain God's love and salvation.

5. Share Christian Resources: Provide resources like books, articles, podcasts, or online sermons that explain the Christian faith and answer common questions.

6. Invite to Church: Invite friends and acquaintances to attend your church services or events. The community and worship experience can be impactful.

7. Pray for Open Doors: Pray for opportunities to share your faith and for receptive hearts. God can open doors for meaningful conversations.

8. Seek Guidance: If you're unsure how to approach someone, seek guidance from your pastor or a more experienced believer.

9. Live a Godly Life: Your actions and lifestyle can speak volumes. Live out your faith authentically, demonstrating the love and character of Christ.

10. Respect Boundaries: Respect people's boundaries and beliefs. Avoid pushiness or coercion in your conversations.

11. Address Questions: Be prepared to answer common questions about Christianity, such as the problem of evil, the reliability of the Bible, and the evidence for the resurrection of Jesus.

12. Share Your Church's Resources: Utilize your church's evangelistic resources, such as tracts or websites, to provide information about Christianity.

13. Small Group Discussions: Host or participate in small group discussions where faith-related topics can be explored openly and honestly.

14. Social Media: Use social media to share faith-related content, personal reflections, and encouraging messages.

15. Attend Outreach Events: Join or organize outreach events or mission trips to reach people with the gospel.

16. Be Patient: Sharing your faith can be a long-term process. Be patient and continue to pray for those you're sharing with.

REMEMBER THAT THE HOLY Spirit plays a crucial role in convicting hearts and drawing people to Christ. Your role is to be a faithful and loving witness. Provide resources like books, articles, or websites that can further explain and support the Christian faith. Some valuable resources include:

Books: Recommend books like "Mere Christianity" by C.S. Lewis, "The Case for Christ" by Lee Strobel, or "The Reason for God" by Timothy Keller.

Websites: Share websites like gotquestions.org, desiringgod.org, or apologetics315.com, which provide answers to common questions about Christianity.

Online Sermons and Podcasts: Direct them to online sermons and podcasts from reputable pastors and theologians, such as John Piper, Ravi Zacharias, or Tim Keller.

Bible Apps: Encourage them to download Bible apps like YouVersion, which offer various Bible translations and reading plans.

Christian Videos: Share video resources like those found on YouTube channels like The Bible Project or Alpha.

Tracts and Pamphlets: Distribute evangelistic tracts or pamphlets that explain the gospel in a concise and clear manner.

By equipping yourself with these resources and using effective communication, you can effectively share your faith and help others on their journey toward Christ.

Authenticity: Authenticity is crucial when sharing your faith. People are more likely to listen to your message if they see your genuine love for Jesus and others.

Building Relationships: Building relationships is a powerful way to share your faith. Invest time in getting to know people, showing care and compassion, and earning their trust.

Listening: Effective communication involves listening as much as speaking. Listen to others' questions, concerns, and stories. This can create opportunities for meaningful conversations about faith.

Sharing Your Story: Your personal testimony is a valuable tool for sharing your faith. Describe how Jesus has made a difference in your life and the transformation you've experienced.

Answering Questions: Be prepared to answer questions about your faith. Study the Bible and deepen your understanding of the core beliefs of Christianity.

Inviting to Church: Inviting someone to your church can be a non-threatening way to introduce them to the Christian community and the teachings of Jesus.

Praying for Others: Praying for others is a powerful way to share your faith. Offer to pray for people's needs and concerns, and share how prayer has impacted your life.

Sharing Resources: Share books, articles, videos, or websites that have been helpful to you in your faith journey. These resources can provide valuable insights and answers to questions.

Being a Light in Your Sphere of Influence

Being a light in your sphere of influence means living out your faith in a way that positively impacts those around you. It's about embodying the teachings of Jesus and demonstrating His love, grace, and truth in your everyday life. Here's a deeper exploration of what it means to be a light in your sphere of influence:

Authentic Faith: Authenticity is key. Live out your faith genuinely, avoiding hypocrisy. When your beliefs align with your actions, you become a credible and compelling witness.

Love and Compassion: Jesus' command to love your neighbor as yourself (Matthew 22:39) is foundational. Show love and compassion to everyone you encounter, regardless of their background, beliefs, or circumstances.

Servant Leadership: Follow Jesus' example of servant leadership (Mark 10:45). Be willing to serve and support others, putting their needs above your own.

Humility: Humility is attractive and disarms pride and arrogance. Recognize that you are a sinner saved by grace, and approach others with humility and grace.

Integrity: Maintain high ethical standards in your personal and professional life. Your integrity speaks volumes about your character and values.

Prayer: Pray for your sphere of influence regularly. Lift up the needs and concerns of those around you, asking God to work in their lives.

Boldness and Grace: Don't shy away from sharing your faith when appropriate but do so with gentleness and respect (1 Peter 3:15). Be prepared to explain the hope you have in Christ.

Lifestyle Evangelism: Let your life be a living testimony. Your choices, priorities, and reactions should reflect your faith. People should see a distinct difference in how you approach life's challenges and joys.

Listen Actively: Be a good listener. Show genuine interest in the stories and struggles of others. Listening provides opportunities to empathize and offer support.

Empathy: Put yourself in others' shoes. Try to understand their perspectives and struggles. Empathy fosters connections and bridges gaps.

Consistency: Consistency in your character and conduct is essential. Whether in good times or bad, people should see a steadfast faith.

Encouragement: Be an encourager. Lift up those who are discouraged or struggling. Your words of hope and affirmation can make a significant impact.

Conflict Resolution: Handle conflicts with grace and reconciliation. Peacemaking reflects the character of Christ.

Generosity: Be generous with your time, resources, and kindness. Acts of generosity demonstrate the selflessness of Christ.

Invitation: Invite people into your faith journey. Share about your church, small group, or faith community, and encourage them to explore their own spiritual path.

Practical Help: Offer practical help to those in need. Acts of service and kindness demonstrate the love of Christ in tangible ways.

Support and Discipleship: Disciple and mentor others in their faith journey. Help them grow spiritually and navigate the challenges of life.

Respect Differences: Respect the diverse beliefs and backgrounds of those in your sphere of influence. Maintain open dialogue while showing respect for differing viewpoints.

Remember that being a light doesn't mean imposing your beliefs on others but rather shining so brightly with love, grace, and truth that others are drawn to the source of your light, which is Christ. Your sphere of influence may include family, friends, colleagues, neighbors, and acquaintances. By living out your faith with authenticity and compassion, you can have a profound and lasting impact on those around you, pointing them toward the love and salvation found in Jesus Christ.

Living a Christ-Centered Life: Your actions and attitudes should reflect the teachings of Jesus. Strive to live a life that stands out as different in a positive way.

Kindness and Compassion: Show kindness and compassion to others. Acts of love and generosity can draw people to Christ.

Modeling Forgiveness: As a disciple, you can model forgiveness by extending grace to others, just as Christ forgave you.

Patience and Grace: Be patient and understanding when others have questions or doubts. Offer grace and remember that faith journeys vary.

The Importance of Prayer

Prayer is a cornerstone of the Christian faith, serving as a direct line of communication between believers and God. It holds immense significance in the life of a disciple for various reasons:

1. **Communion with God:** Prayer fosters an intimate relationship with God, allowing believers to connect with their Creator on a personal level.

2. **Guidance and Direction:** In moments of uncertainty, prayer offers guidance as believers seek God's wisdom and discernment.

3. **Strength and Comfort:** During times of trial and suffering, prayer provides strength and comfort, akin to Jesus' solace in Gethsemane.

4. **Confession and Repentance:** Prayer enables confession and repentance, cleansing the heart and maintaining a close relationship with God.

5. **Intercession for Others:** It extends beyond personal needs, allowing believers to intercede for others and demonstrate love and compassion.

6. **Gratitude and Praise:** Prayer is a means of expressing gratitude and praise, reminding believers of God's goodness and faithfulness.

7. **Spiritual Transformation:** It facilitates spiritual growth and transformation, renewing the mind through prayer and the study of God's Word.

8. **Spiritual Warfare:** Believers engage in spiritual warfare through prayer, seeking God's protection and guidance in the face of spiritual opposition.

9. **Alignment with God's Will:** Prayer aligns desires with God's will, submitting to His plan for life.

10. **Faith Building:** Through answered prayers, believers experience God's faithfulness, strengthening their trust in Him.

11. **Stress Relief:** Prayer provides peace that surpasses understanding, allowing believers to cast anxieties upon God.

12. **Expression of Dependence:** It acknowledges dependence on God for guidance, provision, and intervention.

13. **Fellowship with Believers:** Praying together fosters unity among believers and reinforces their shared commitment to Christ.

14. **Thanksgiving:** Prayer encourages gratitude in all circumstances, promoting a positive perspective.

Resources for Deepening Your Prayer Life:

1. **"The Power of Prayer"** by E.M. Bounds: This classic book explores the transformative impact of prayer and offers insights into developing a powerful prayer life.
2. **"Prayer: Experiencing Awe and Intimacy with God"** by Timothy Keller: Keller's book delves into the theology and practice of prayer, helping believers connect with God in deeper ways.
3. **Prayer Journals:** Keeping a prayer journal can aid in tracking prayer requests, recording answered prayers, and fostering reflection on your spiritual journey.
4. **Prayer Apps:** Utilize apps like "PrayerMate" or "Echo Prayer" to organize prayer requests and maintain a consistent prayer routine.
5. **Prayer Retreats:** Consider attending a prayer retreat or organizing one with your church or small group to focus on deepening your prayer life.
6. **Prayer Partners:** Partner with a fellow believer for regular prayer and accountability, enhancing your prayer experience.
7. **Scripture:** Incorporate relevant Bible verses into your prayers, drawing inspiration from passages like the Lord's Prayer (Matthew 6:9-13) or Paul's prayers in Ephesians (Ephesians 1:15-23, 3:14-21).
8. **Online Prayer Communities:** Engage with online prayer communities or join prayer groups within your local church to pray collectively for various needs.
9. **Biographies and Testimonies:** Reading biographies or testimonies of individuals with powerful prayer lives can provide inspiration and practical insights.
10. **Prayer Workshops and Seminars:** Attend workshops or seminars on prayer to deepen your understanding and

practice.

Remember that prayer is a dynamic and deeply personal journey. While resources can enhance your prayer life, the most important aspect is consistent communication with God, developing a vibrant and enduring relationship with your heavenly Father.

Praying for Opportunities: Pray for opportunities to share your faith and for the people in your sphere of influence.

Praying for Hearts to Be Opened: Pray for God to open the hearts and minds of those you encounter, that they may be receptive to the gospel.

Seeking Guidance: Seek God's guidance in your efforts to share your faith. Ask for wisdom and discernment in your interactions.

In this chapter, we have explored the importance of sharing your faith and being a light in your sphere of influence. As a disciple, you are called to share the life-changing message of Jesus Christ with others. By living authentically, building relationships, answering questions, and demonstrating the love of Christ, you can effectively fulfill the Great Commission and help others come to know and follow Jesus.

Chapter 9: Continual Growth

DISCIPLESHIP IS NOT a destination; it's a lifelong journey of growth and transformation. In this final chapter, we will emphasize the importance of continually seeking God, deepening your relationship with Him, and striving to become more like Jesus.

The Journey of Lifelong Growth

The path of discipleship is a lifelong journey marked by continuous growth and transformation. As a disciple of Jesus, you are on a dynamic and evolving quest to become more like Him. Here are key aspects of this journey:

1. **Seeking God's Presence:** The journey begins with an earnest desire to seek God's presence daily. It involves setting aside time for prayer, meditation, and reflection to deepen your relationship with Him.

2. **Studying God's Word:** Lifelong growth entails a commitment to studying and meditating on God's Word. The Bible serves as your guide, revealing God's character, His will, and the principles by which you should live.

3. **Embracing Discipleship Principles:** Continually apply the principles of discipleship discussed in this book, such as love, forgiveness, compassion, and service, to your daily life.

4. **Living a Life of Repentance:** Acknowledge that growth often involves recognizing areas of sin and repenting. This ongoing process leads to transformation and greater conformity to the image of Christ.

5. **Spiritual Disciplines:** Incorporate spiritual disciplines like fasting, solitude, and worship into your routine. These practices foster spiritual growth and intimacy with God.

6. **Community and Fellowship:** Continue to engage in Christian community and fellowship. Regularly gathering with other believers provides support, accountability, and opportunities for growth.

7. **Sharing Your Faith:** Actively share your faith with others and disciple new believers. This not only fulfills the Great Commission but also deepens your own understanding of God's Word.

8. **Serving Others:** As you grow, use your gifts and talents to serve others selflessly. Living a life of service reflects the love of Christ and contributes to your spiritual development.

9. **Facing Challenges with Resilience:** Understand that challenges and trials are part of the journey. Approach them with resilience, relying on God's grace and strength to overcome.

10. **Rejoicing in God's Grace:** Continually marvel at the grace of God. Let His unmerited favor and forgiveness inspire gratitude and humility in your heart.

11. **Evolving Faith:** Recognize that your faith may evolve and deepen over time. Embrace a faith that is willing to question, learn, and adapt while holding firm to the unchanging truths of the gospel.

12. **Mentoring and Discipling Others:** As you grow, mentor and disciple others who are earlier in their journey. Invest in their growth and pass on the wisdom and knowledge you've gained.

13. **Reflect and Adjust:** Regularly take time to reflect on your spiritual journey. Adjust your course as needed, seeking to align your life more closely with Christ's example.

14. **Prayer for Continual Growth:** Pray for God's guidance and empowerment in your quest for growth. Ask Him to reveal areas where you can mature and become more Christlike.

Remember that the journey of lifelong growth is not about achieving perfection but about becoming progressively conformed to the image of Christ. It's a journey marked by grace, faith, and the continuous work of the Holy Spirit within you. Embrace the process, and may your pursuit of Christlikeness be a source of joy and fulfillment throughout your life.

Transformation: Discipleship involves ongoing transformation. Romans 12:2 encourages you to "be transformed by the renewing of your mind." As you continue to follow Jesus, your character, attitudes, and behaviors should increasingly align with His teachings.

A Deeper Relationship: Your relationship with God is dynamic and deepening. Just as in any relationship, communication, trust, and intimacy with God can grow over time.

Commitment to Spiritual Disciplines

Spiritual disciplines are practices that cultivate a deeper relationship with God, foster spiritual growth, and nurture the life of a disciple. Committing to these disciplines is vital for ongoing spiritual development. Here are some key disciplines and resources to help you in your journey:

1. **Prayer:** Develop a consistent and meaningful prayer life. Resources like "The Circle Maker" by Mark Batterson or "Prayer: Experiencing Awe and Intimacy with God" by Timothy Keller can deepen your understanding of prayer.

2. **Bible Study:** Engage in regular Bible study and meditation. Consider using resources like the "YouVersion Bible App" with various reading plans or study guides like "Life Application Study Bible" to enhance your study.

3. **Fasting:** Incorporate fasting into your spiritual life. "A Hunger for God" by John Piper provides insights into the spiritual discipline of fasting.

4. **Worship:** Engage in heartfelt worship through music, liturgy, and gratitude. Explore worship songs and albums from artists like Hillsong, Bethel Music, or Chris Tomlin.

5. **Fellowship:** Prioritize regular participation in a local church or faith community. Join small groups or Bible studies within your church to deepen your connections.

6. **Service:** Find opportunities for serving others in your community or through church ministries. Books like "The Purpose Driven Life" by Rick Warren can inspire a life of service.

7. **Silence and Solitude:** Make space for silence and solitude to hear God's voice. Books like "Celebration of Discipline" by Richard J. Foster offer insights into these disciplines.

8. **Giving:** Develop a habit of generous giving, not only financially but also of your time and talents. "The Treasure Principle" by Randy Alcorn provides a perspective on stewardship and generosity.

9. **Meditation:** Practice Christian meditation on Scripture and the character of God. Resources like "Meditation and Communion with God" by John Owen explore this discipline.

10. **Journaling:** Keep a spiritual journal to record your thoughts, prayers, and reflections on your faith journey.

11. **Accountability:** Establish accountability relationships with trusted fellow believers who can support your growth and hold you accountable in your walk with Christ.

12. **Mission and Evangelism:** Actively engage in sharing the gospel with others. "The Master Plan of Evangelism" by Robert E. Coleman is a classic resource on evangelism and disciple-making.

13. **Sabbath Rest:** Observe a regular day of rest and reflection. "The Rest of God" by Mark Buchanan explores the concept of Sabbath rest.

14. **Study of Christian Classics:** Explore classic Christian literature and theology from authors like Augustine, Thomas Aquinas, C.S. Lewis, and A.W. Tozer.

15. **Prayer Retreats:** Attend prayer retreats or workshops that focus on deepening your prayer life and spiritual disciplines.

Remember that spiritual disciplines are not about legalism but about drawing closer to God and nurturing your relationship with Him. They can be adapted to your unique personality and circumstances.

Approach them with a humble heart and a desire for growth, allowing the Holy Spirit to guide you in your practice of these disciplines.

Prayer: Regular and heartfelt prayer keeps your connection with God strong. As you pray, share your joys, sorrows, hopes, and fears with Him.

Scripture Study: Consistent study of the Bible deepens your understanding of God's Word and His plan for your life. Psalm 119:105 reminds you that "Your word is a lamp to my feet and a light to my path."

Worship: Engaging in meaningful worship helps you connect with God on a spiritual and emotional level. Worship is more than singing; it's a posture of the heart.

Fellowship: Continue to actively participate in your faith community. As you gather with fellow believers, you learn, grow, and encourage one another.

Navigating Challenges and Doubts

Challenges and doubts are an inevitable part of the discipleship journey. However, they can also be opportunities for growth and deepening your faith. Here are resources and strategies to help you navigate these challenges:

1. **Spiritual Guidance:** Seek guidance from a pastor, spiritual mentor, or counselor who can provide biblical wisdom and perspective on your challenges and doubts.

2. **Prayer and Meditation:** Engage in focused prayer and meditation on Scripture to seek clarity and peace amidst doubts. The book "Disappointment with God" by Philip Yancey can be helpful.

3. **Community Support:** Share your doubts and struggles with trusted members of your faith community. Sometimes, discussing your concerns with others can provide valuable insights and support.

4. **Study Apologetics:** Explore resources in Christian apologetics to address intellectual doubts. "Mere Christianity" by C.S. Lewis and "The Case for Christ" by Lee Strobel are excellent resources.

5. **Read Biographies:** Reading biographies of Christians who faced doubts and challenges can be inspiring. Consider "Surprised by Joy" by C.S. Lewis or "The Hiding Place" by Corrie ten Boom.

6. **Journaling:** Keep a spiritual journal to document your doubts, questions, and moments of clarity. Reflecting on your journey can reveal patterns and growth.

7. **Christian Counseling:** If doubts or challenges become overwhelming, consider seeking Christian counseling or therapy to address deeper emotional or psychological issues.

8. **Theology and Apologetics Courses:** Enroll in theology or apologetics courses offered by reputable institutions or online platforms to deepen your understanding of Christian beliefs.

---

9. **Reading the Psalms:** The Psalms often express the full range of human emotions, including doubt and lament. Reading and meditating on the Psalms can be comforting in times of struggle.

10. **Stay Connected to God:** Even when facing doubts, continue to engage in prayer, worship, and Bible study. Sometimes, it's during these practices that doubts are resolved.

11. **Reflect on Your Faith Journey:** Periodically reflect on your faith journey, acknowledging how God has guided you through past challenges and doubts. This can provide assurance for the present.

12. **Join a Doubt-Friendly Group:** Some churches or online communities have groups dedicated to discussing doubts and challenging questions in a supportive environment.

13. **Reading the Book of Job:** The book of Job addresses profound questions about suffering and faith. Reading and studying it can provide insights into navigating doubts.

14. **Cultivate Resilience:** Develop emotional and spiritual resilience by focusing on the foundational truths of your faith and the assurance of God's love.

Remember that doubts are a natural part of faith, and many great Christian thinkers and leaders have faced them. Embrace your doubts as opportunities for growth and seek God's guidance and wisdom in navigating them. Ultimately, a deeper and more mature faith can emerge from the process of grappling with doubts.

Perseverance: Challenges and doubts are a normal part of the discipleship journey. Persevere in your faith, knowing that God is with you in the valleys and on the mountaintops.

Seeking Answers: When doubts arise, seek answers through prayer, study, and discussion with trusted mentors or fellow believers.

Trust in God's Faithfulness: Remember God's faithfulness in your past experiences. This can provide assurance and strengthen your trust in Him during challenging times.

Serving Others

Serving others is a fundamental aspect of discipleship, reflecting the love and selflessness of Jesus. Here are some insights and strategies to guide you in your service to others:

1. **Serve with Love:** Jesus taught that the greatest commandment is to love God and love your neighbor as yourself (Matthew 22:36-40). Approach service with a genuine love for others.

2. **Identify Needs:** Be attentive to the needs of those around you, both in your local community and beyond. Seek opportunities to meet physical, emotional, and spiritual needs.

3. **Discover Your Gifts:** Identify your unique gifts, talents, and abilities, and use them for service. As mentioned earlier in this book, explore resources and assessments to help you discover your spiritual gifts.

4. **Start Small:** You don't have to start with grand gestures. Small acts of kindness and service can have a significant impact. Start where you are with what you have.

Join a Ministry: Get involved in a church or community ministry that aligns with your passions and talents. This provides structure and support for your service efforts.

6. **Consistency Matters:** Regular and consistent service often has a more profound impact than sporadic efforts. Commit to ongoing service rather than one-time projects.

7. **Collaborate:** Team up with others to serve together. Collaborative efforts can be more effective and enjoyable.

8. **Pray for Discernment:** Seek God's guidance in your service endeavors. Pray for discernment to understand where He wants you to focus your efforts.

9. **Learn and Adapt:** Continuously learn about the needs of the people you serve and adapt your approach as circumstances change.

10. **Listen Actively:** When serving others, practice active listening. Pay attention to their stories, concerns, and feelings.

11. **Empower Others:** Encourage and empower those you serve to become self-sufficient and independent when appropriate. Provide tools and resources for long-term growth.

12. **Practice Humility:** Approach service with humility, recognizing that you are not the savior but a vessel through which God's love flows.

13. **Measure Impact:** Assess the impact of your service efforts to ensure they are making a positive difference. Use feedback and evaluations to refine your approach.

14. **Teach and Mentor:** Share your knowledge and skills with others. Mentor and disciple those you serve, empowering them to grow.

15. **Extend Grace:** Understand that not every act of service will be perfect, and challenges may arise. Extend grace to yourself and others in the process.

16. **Reflect and Celebrate:** Take time to reflect on your service experiences and celebrate the moments of transformation and impact.

17. **Global Missions:** Consider engaging in global missions to serve in different cultural contexts. Organizations like "Missions Door" or "World Vision" offer opportunities for international service.

18. **Rest and Self-Care:** While service is important, remember to prioritize rest and self-care to prevent burnout. You cannot serve effectively if you are physically and emotionally depleted.

Serving others is a tangible expression of your faith and love for God. It brings joy, fulfillment, and a deeper sense of purpose to your discipleship journey. By following these principles and strategies, you can make a meaningful impact in the lives of those you serve while growing in your relationship with Christ.

Expanding Your Impact: As you grow in your faith, your capacity to serve others also expands. You can make a more significant impact in your community and the world.

Compassion and Love: Deepening your relationship with God should result in a greater outpouring of love and compassion for those around you.

Emulating Christ's Character

Emulating the character of Christ is the core of discipleship. Here are insights and strategies to help you become more like Jesus in your daily life:

1. **Deepen Your Love for God:** Emulating Christ's character starts with a deep and genuine love for God. Cultivate this love through prayer, worship, and spending time in His presence.

2. **Study the Life of Jesus:** Immerse yourself in the Gospels to understand how Jesus lived and interacted with others. Study His teachings, actions, and attitudes.

3. **Meditate on the Sermon on the Mount:** The Sermon on the Mount in Matthew 5-7 contains Jesus' foundational teachings. Reflect on these teachings and seek to embody them in your life.

4. **Practice Humility:** Jesus displayed profound humility, even washing His disciples' feet (John 13:1-17). Cultivate humility in your interactions with others.

5. **Love Your Neighbor:** Jesus' command to love your neighbor as yourself (Mark 12:31) is central to emulating His character. Look for opportunities to show love and kindness to those around you.

6. **Extend Forgiveness:** Forgive others as Christ forgave you (Colossians 3:13). Let go of bitterness and resentment, offering forgiveness and reconciliation when possible.

7. **Practice Compassion:** Follow Jesus' example of compassion toward the marginalized and hurting (Matthew 9:36). Be empathetic and show kindness to those in need.

8. **Serve Selflessly:** As mentioned in earlier chapters, serve others selflessly, reflecting Christ's sacrificial service (Mark 10:45).

9. **Seek God's Will:** Jesus always sought the Father's will (John 6:38). Strive to align your desires and decisions with God's will through prayer and discernment.

10. **Embrace Obedience:** Obedience to God's commandments is a hallmark of discipleship (John 14:23). Seek to obey His Word and follow His guidance.

11. **Cultivate a Prayerful Life:** Jesus often withdrew to pray and seek God's guidance (Mark 1:35). Make prayer a regular part of your life to stay connected with God.

12. **Respond with Grace:** When faced with difficult situations or conflicts, respond with grace and a Christlike attitude (Colossians 4:6).

13. **Practice Self-Control:** Self-control is a fruit of the Spirit (Galatians 5:22-23). Exercise self-control in your actions, thoughts, and words.

14. **Live with Integrity:** Jesus lived with unwavering integrity. Be truthful, honest, and trustworthy in all your interactions.

15. **Build Healthy Relationships:** Jesus had meaningful relationships with His disciples. Cultivate healthy, supportive relationships with fellow believers.

16. **Be a Light:** Be a light in your sphere of influence, reflecting the love and truth of Christ (Matthew 5:14-16).

17. **Reflect on Your Progress:** Periodically reflect on your journey to emulate Christ's character. Celebrate areas of growth and identify areas that need improvement.

18. **Seek the Holy Spirit's Guidance:** Rely on the Holy Spirit to empower and transform you into Christ's likeness (Galatians 5:16).

19. **Practice Patience:** Patience is a virtue that Christ exemplified. Be patient with yourself and others as you grow in Christlikeness.

20. **Persevere:** Discipleship is a lifelong journey. Persevere in your pursuit of emulating Christ's character, knowing that He is with you every step of the way.

Emulating Christ's character is a lifelong endeavor, and no one achieves it perfectly. However, the journey itself is transformative and draws you closer to the heart of God. Continually seek His guidance and rely on His grace as you strive to become more like Jesus in every aspect of your life.

The Ultimate Goal: The ultimate goal of discipleship is to become more like Jesus. Philippians 2:5 encourages you to "have this mind among yourselves, which is yours in Christ Jesus."

Fruit of the Spirit: Galatians 5:22-23 describes the fruit of the Spirit, including love, joy, peace, patience, kindness, goodness, faithfulness, gentleness, and self-control. Strive to manifest these qualities in your life.

The fruit of the Spirit, as described in Galatians 5:22-23, are qualities and virtues that reflect the character of Christ. Let's explore the fruit and gain insights into how they can be cultivated in your life:

Love: Love is the foundational fruit, and it encompasses selfless affection, care, and goodwill towards others. It's not just an emotion but a choice to act in the best interest of others, even when it's challenging. Love reflects God's very nature (1 John 4:7-8).

Insight: Love starts with an understanding of how deeply you are loved by God. As you grasp the depth of His love for you, you can extend that love to others.

Joy: Joy is more than temporary happiness; it's a deep-seated gladness that comes from knowing Christ. It's not dependent on circumstances but rooted in your relationship with God. Jesus prayed for His followers to have His joy (John 15:11).

Insight: Cultivate joy by focusing on the hope and salvation found in Christ, even in difficult times. Joy arises from trust in God's sovereignty.

Peace: Peace involves inner tranquility and harmony with God. It's a sense of wholeness and well-being that transcends external turmoil. Jesus is the Prince of Peace (Isaiah 9:6).

Insight: Seek peace through prayer and surrender. Trust that God is in control, and His peace will guard your heart and mind (Philippians 4:6-7).

Patience: Patience is the ability to endure difficulties and hardships with a calm and steady spirit. It reflects God's patience with humanity. God's patience leads to repentance (Romans 2:4).

Insight: Practice patience by trusting God's timing. Remember that God's plans are perfect, even if they don't align with your timetable.

Kindness: Kindness is an attitude of compassion and goodwill towards others. It involves genuine care and a desire to alleviate suffering. God's kindness leads to repentance (Romans 2:4).

Insight: Look for opportunities to show kindness in your daily interactions, even in small ways. Acts of kindness can have a profound impact.

Goodness: Goodness is the quality of moral excellence and integrity. It involves doing what is right and just. God is the ultimate source of goodness (Psalm 34:8).

Insight: Strive for goodness by aligning your actions with God's Word and ethical principles. Make choices that reflect God's righteousness.

Faithfulness: Faithfulness is reliability and loyalty in relationships. It mirrors God's faithfulness to His promises. God remains faithful even when we are faithless (2 Timothy 2:13).

Insight: Cultivate faithfulness by honoring your commitments and staying true to your word. Be consistent in your relationship with God and others.

Gentleness: Gentleness involves humility, meekness, and a gentle demeanor, even in the face of conflict or opposition. It reflects Christ's gentle and humble heart (Matthew 11:29).

Insight: Practice gentleness by seeking to understand others, showing empathy, and responding with a calm spirit rather than defensiveness.

Self-Control: Self-control is the ability to exercise restraint over your desires and impulses. It allows you to make wise choices and avoid sin. It's a fruit that helps you resist temptation (1 Corinthians 10:13).

Insight: Develop self-control through prayer, accountability, and reliance on the Holy Spirit. Recognize your weaknesses and trust in God's strength.

As you nurture the fruit in your life, remember that it's the Holy Spirit who produces them in you. Stay connected to God through prayer, study of His Word, and a surrendered heart, and you will see the fruit will grow and flourish in your discipleship journey.

A LIFE OF LOVE: Above all, cultivate a life characterized by love. Jesus said in John 13:35, "By this, all people will know that you are my disciples if you have love for one another."

The Never-Ending Journey

The journey of discipleship is never-ending. It's a lifelong pursuit of becoming more like Jesus, continually seeking God, and growing in your faith. Here are some key insights about this ongoing journey:

1. **Dynamic Growth:** Discipleship is not a static state but a dynamic process. Your faith should constantly evolve as you deepen your relationship with God.

2. **Deeper Understanding:** As you mature in your faith, you'll gain a deeper understanding of God's Word, His character, and His will for your life.

3. **Facing New Challenges:** New challenges and questions will arise as you progress. Embrace these moments as opportunities for growth and exploration.

4. **Grace for Imperfection:** Understand that you will never reach perfection in this life. God's grace covers your imperfections, and He continues to work in you.

5. **A Journey of Transformation:** Discipleship transforms every aspect of your life—your thoughts, attitudes, behaviors, and relationships.

6. **Perseverance:** There will be times of trial and testing. Perseverance is key; keep moving forward, even when the path is difficult.

7. **Community and Support:** Surround yourself with a faith community that encourages and supports your growth. Seek accountability and mentorship.

8. **Serving Others:** Service remains an integral part of your journey. It not only impacts others but also deepens your understanding of Christ's love.

9. **A Closer Walk with God:** The goal of discipleship is to draw closer to God. It's about knowing Him intimately and being conformed to His image (Romans 8:29).

10. **Seeking God's Will:** Continually seek God's will for your life. As you do, you'll discover new callings and assignments.

11. **Celebrate Milestones:** Celebrate your growth milestones. Reflect on how far you've come, and the ways God has shaped you.

12. **Stay Humble:** Maintain humility throughout your journey. Recognize that you are always a learner in God's hands.

13. **Deepening Prayer Life:** Invest in your prayer life. It's your direct line to God and a source of guidance and strength.

14. **Study and Learning:** Keep studying God's Word and learning about Him. There is always more to discover.

15. **Teaching and Sharing:** As you grow, share your knowledge and experiences with others. Disciple others on their journey.

16. **Remember Your Purpose:** Always remember that your purpose is to glorify God and make His love known to the world.

17. **Trust in God's Faithfulness:** Trust that God is faithful to complete the work He began in you (Philippians 1:6).

18. **Embrace Change:** Be open to change and transformation, even if it takes you out of your comfort zone.

19. **Joyful Anticipation:** Approach each day of discipleship with joyful anticipation, knowing that God has wonderful things in store for you.

20. **Eternal Perspective:** Keep an eternal perspective. Remember that this life is just a part of your journey toward an eternity with God.

Your discipleship journey is a profound and rewarding adventure. It's a never-ending pursuit of God's heart, a continual transformation into Christ's likeness, and a fulfilling way to live out your faith in a broken world. Embrace the journey with faith, hope, and love, knowing that God is with you every step of the way.

Embrace the Process: Discipleship is a never-ending journey. Embrace the process of growth and transformation, knowing that you are becoming more like Christ with each step.

Celebrate Progress: Celebrate your progress and victories along the way and be patient with yourself in areas where growth may be slower.

Continue Seeking God: Continue seeking God with a hungry heart. As you do, you will find that the journey of discipleship is not only transformative but also a source of profound joy, purpose, and fulfillment.

In this final chapter, we have emphasized the importance of continual growth in your discipleship journey. Remember that discipleship is a lifelong pursuit of deepening your relationship with God and becoming more like Jesus. It's a journey of transformation, marked by prayer, study, worship, fellowship, and a commitment to serving others. As you continue to seek God and follow Him with your whole heart, may you experience the abundant life and rich spiritual growth that discipleship offers.

Conclusion

"So You've Been Baptized, What's Next: The Road to Discipleship" has been your guide to the exciting and fulfilling journey of following Jesus. It's a path that may have its challenges, but it's also a path filled with purpose, meaning, and abundant life.

As you've explored the rich symbolism of baptism, delved into the foundational aspects of discipleship, embraced the teachings of Jesus, understood the power of grace, learned to live a life of service, faced challenges and trials, prioritized community and fellowship, shared your faith, and committed to continual growth, you've embarked on a journey that will transform your life.

Remember, you are not alone on this journey. God is with you every step of the way, guiding, empowering, and sustaining you. Your faith community and fellow disciples are here to support and encourage you.

As you continue your discipleship journey, may you experience the deep joy and fulfillment that come from following Jesus. May you be a beacon of light, love, and hope in your sphere of influence. And may your life be a testimony to the transformative power of God's grace and the beauty of a life fully surrendered to Him.

Keep walking the road of discipleship with confidence and joy, knowing that it leads to a life that reflects the character of Christ and brings glory to God.

Don't miss out!

Visit the website below and you can sign up to receive emails whenever Minister Jeremy B. Sims publishes a new book. There's no charge and no obligation.

https://books2read.com/r/B-A-AHMAB-LZDOC

BOOKS 2 READ

Connecting independent readers to independent writers.

Did you love *So You've Been Baptized, What's Next: The Road to Discipleship*? Then you should read *From Milk to Meat: The Journey of Spiritual Maturity*[1] by Minister Jeremy B. Sims!

[2]

In the annals of spiritual literature, few metaphors are as potent as the transformation from milk to meat. A tender infant, entirely dependent, begins its life nourished by milk. Yet, as that child grows, matures, and gains strength, its diet must evolve. Milk remains fundamental but is supplemented, and eventually replaced, by more substantial sustenance. Similarly, the spiritual journey of a believer often begins with foundational teachings—the "milk" of spiritual knowledge. But to truly flourish and become robust in one's faith, one must transition to the "meat"—the deeper, more profound truths.

---

1. https://books2read.com/u/bpY9wz

2. https://books2read.com/u/bpY9wz

Also by Minister Jeremy B. Sims

Stop Blaming the Adversary: It's You!
From Milk to Meat: The Journey of Spiritual Maturity
So You've Been Baptized, What's Next: The Road to Discipleship
Why Worrying is A Waste: The Biblical Perspective